MEXICAN COOKING
FOR BEGINNERS

Also by Helene Siegel

Italian Cooking for Beginners
Chinese Cooking for Beginners

COAUTHOR

Ma Cuisine Cooking School Cookbook
City Cuisine

THE ETHNIC KITCHEN

MEXICAN COOKING FOR BEGINNERS

MORE THAN 65 RECIPES FOR THE EAGER COOK

HELENE SIEGEL

ILLUSTRATIONS BY YAN NASCIMBENE

HarperCollins*Publishers*

HarperCollins books may be purchased for
educational, business, or sales promotional use.
For information, please write: Special Markets
Department, HarperCollins Publishers, Inc.,
10 East 53rd Street, New York, NY 10022.

FIRST EDITION

Designed by Stephanie Tevonian

Library of Congress Cataloging-in-Publication Data
Siegel, Helene.
    Mexican cooking for beginners : More than 65
recipes for the eager cook / Helene Siegel.—1st ed.
        p.   cm.   —(The Ethnic kitchen)
    Includes bibliographical references and index.
    ISBN 0-06-016432-8
    1. Cookery, Mexican. I. Title. II. Series:
Siegel, Helene. Ethnic kitchen.
TX716.M4S54 1992   92-53374
641.5972—dc20

93 94 95 96 97 DT/RRD 10 9 8 7 6 5 4 3 2 1

For baby Andrew—may he always eat well

CONTENTS

Contents

Thanks to the following restaurants for contributing their valuable recipes: La Cabanita of Glendale, California, Merida of Pasadena, Border Grill of Santa Monica, and Hotel Presidente of Cozumel, Mexico.

To Marianne Borgardt, Helen Weston, Mike and Trudi Krose, and Doug Bergstresser for their help in tracking down sources and defining tastes.

To Stephanie Tevonian and Yan Nascimbene for excellent book design and superb illustration, respectively.

And to Eleanore Rohrlich, Rose Levey, and Maria Luisa Gomez for helping at home so that I could go to Mexico and taste the real thing. Thanks.

How to Cook Mexican Food

To begin cooking real Mexican food at home, you may first have to forget. Forget about soggy enchiladas, crisp ground beef tacos, Day-Glo orange nachos, and prefab salsas.

Real Mexican food is something much finer and deeper.

It is cakey, soft corn tortillas, slightly charred from the griddle and folded over a square of string cheese and a single squash blossom. It is finely puréed silky vegetable soups of corn, carrots, or broccoli and earthy pork and hominy stews, thickened perhaps with the gelatin from a stewed calf's foot or pig's cheeks. It can be the simplest grilled red snapper punctuated with slivers of garlic and wedges of lime or the most complex Oaxacan mole, a fiesta dish with an ingredient list thirty items long. It can be as mouth-searingly hot as the chile habanero or as cool and refreshing as mango ices. It is spicy and adventurous, intense and elegant, rich and diverse. But mostly it is misunderstood outside its own country.

Good, simple Mexican home cooking is really quite easy to understand. It depends upon very few ingredients, none of them particularly esoteric or expensive. Tomatoes, onion, garlic, and two or three types of chile peppers are the basis for several salsas. Packaged corn tortillas, cheese, eggs, rice and beans with bits of chicken, beef, or pork form a repertoire of soul-satisfying small meals that make excellent weeknight suppers. (These rustic foods have the added virtue of being inexpensive sources of protein. The combinations of corn and beans and rice and beans eaten in the same day provide as much protein as a serving of meat.) Inexpensive cuts of meat are

EITHER COOKED QUICKLY ON THE GRILL OR BRAISED UNTIL TENDER IN A SLOW OVEN.

THIS EASY MEXICAN KITCHEN RELIES ON ONLY THREE BASIC HERBS: CILANTRO, OREGANO, AND EPAZOTE AND A SMALL SHELF OF GROUND, DRIED SPICES: CINNAMON, CUMIN, ANISEED, CLOVE, AND BLACK PEPPER. ALL, EXCEPT THE EPAZOTE, CAN BE FOUND IN ANY WELL-STOCKED URBAN SUPERMARKET. LIME, ORANGE, AND GRAPEFRUIT JUICES, AVAILABLE YEAR-ROUND AT SUPERMARKETS, ARE USED GENEROUSLY AS SEASONINGS AND MARINADES.

MEXICAN COOKING TECHNIQUES ARE LIKEWISE ACCESSIBLE, ALTHOUGH THEY DO ASK THE COOK TO SET ASIDE CERTAIN PRECONCEPTIONS ABOUT "GOOD" COOKING. THERE IS AN ELEMENTAL QUALITY ABOUT THIS COOKING BORN OF THE MARRIAGE OF ANCIENT INDIAN PEOPLES AND THEIR SPANISH CONQUERORS THAT HAS REMAINED UNCHANGED. INGREDIENTS ARE CHARRED DIRECTLY ON A GAS FLAME OR IN A DRY SKILLET. SAUCE MAKING CONSISTS OF PURÉEING INGREDIENTS AND THEN QUICKLY SIZZLING THEM DOWN IN A PAN. THERE IS NOTHING FINICKY ABOUT IT. JUST REMEMBER THAT BURNED IS NOT NECESSARILY BAD AND SAUCE IS SOMETHING TO APPLY WITH A GENEROUS HAND RATHER THAN IN MEASURED DOLLOPS AND YOU ARE OFF TO A GOOD, AUTHENTIC START.

AS FAR AS AUTHENTICITY IS CONCERNED, I HAVE TAKEN SOME LIBERTIES, ACCORDING TO MY GRINGA TASTES. SINCE I DON'T LIKE MY FOOD EXCEPTIONALLY HOT, I HAVE USED CHILE PEPPERS (AND THEIR SEEDS AND VEINS) WITH MORE RESTRAINT THAN MOST MEXICANS WOULD APPROVE OF. IF YOU HAVE BUILT UP A TOLERANCE FOR CHILES OR ARE JUST A NATURAL-BORN CHILE LOVER, PUMP UP THE CHILES AS DESIRED. I HAVE ALSO DONE WITHOUT LARD IN ALL BUT ONE RECIPE, SINCE I HAVE A PREJUDICE AGAINST ADDING THAT PARTICULAR FAT TO MY ARTERIES RIGHT NOW. THERE IS NO

QUESTION LARD WILL ADD A MORE AUTHENTIC FLAVOR TO REFRIED BEANS, FRIED CORN TORTILLA DISHES, AND CERTAIN MEAT AND POULTRY DISHES. FEEL FREE TO SUBSTITUTE IT FOR THE OIL OR BUTTER OTHERWISE CALLED FOR. IF IT IS STILL GREATER AUTHENTICITY AND WEIRDER INGREDIENTS YOU ARE AFTER, YOU ARE PROBABLY READY TO GRADUATE TO ONE OF THE BOOKS LISTED AT THE BACK OF THIS VOLUME.

THE FOODS INCLUDED HERE GIVE A SMALL TASTE OF THE REGIONAL DIVERSITY THAT CHARACTERIZES TRUE MEXICAN COOKING. THIS IS WONDERFUL, UNPRETENTIOUS HOME-BASED COOKING CREATED BY WOMEN TO FEED LARGE FAMILIES WITH EVEN LARGER APPETITES. I THINK YOU WILL FIND IT HAS A COMFORTABLE PLACE IN YOUR OWN KITCHEN.

A FEW TECHNIQUES FOR THE NOVICE

ROASTING OR TOASTING tomatoes, onion, garlic, chile peppers, and spices before they are combined with other ingredients is *the* identifying characteristic of Mexican cooking. It imparts a smoky quality, which, along with an occasional sweet touch from cinnamon or nuts and the obligatory fire from chiles, is responsible for the complex earthiness of much Mexican food.

To roast tomatoes, preheat the broiler and line a baking tray with aluminum foil, both to catch the juices and to facilitate cleaning up. Place the tomatoes on the tray close to the heat and broil, using tongs to turn occasionally, until the skins are charred all over, about 15 minutes. Set the tray aside to cool before handling and then follow instructions concerning the skins and cores. They are not always discarded.

Onions, in their skins, *can be roasted in the same fashion under the broiler.* Or they can be charred over a high flame in a dry, cast-iron skillet. In either case, the blackened skins are discarded.

Garlic cloves are also easily toasted in a dry pan. The results are delicious. Just add the cloves, in their skins, to a small dry skillet over high heat. Cook, turning occasionally and pressing down with tongs to blacken evenly, about 7 minutes. When the cloves cool down, you can peel by crushing with the flat side of a heavy blade. The garlic should be soft with uneven brown patches.

Dry whole spices and seeds roast quickly in a dry pan over low heat. Just shake the pan and watch them carefully since they burn quickly.

Roasting chile peppers, which you may know a little bit about from roasting bell peppers for Italian cooking, will be discussed in the section on handling chiles.

SAUCE MAKING is not a highly technical activity in the Mexican kitchen. The uncooked salsas demand nothing more than a willing chopping arm, and the cooked sauces do not demand much more. The basic technique calls for roughly chopping the ingredients (which may or may not have been first roasted) and then combining them in a blender, where they are puréed. Some oil is then heated in a pot and the purée is poured in, sizzled, and simmered until done, which often happens quickly.

TOMATOES, ONION, AND CHILES are the basis of a number of sauces, soups, and braised dishes. In foods where the combination dominates, the dish is said to be cooked "mexicana" style.

LIME JUICE squirted on grilled fish, poultry, beef, or pork, as well as soups, salads, and corn tortilla dishes gives an instant Mexican flavor.

TORTILLAS are eaten like bread, as a starch accompaniment, but they also are called for as an ingredient in preparing other foods. Corn tortillas are crisp-fried to form chips and strips for garnishing soups and the crisp shells called *tostadas* that serve as a plate for salads; they are softened and dipped in sauce to form *enchiladas*, fried and folded over cheese to form *quesadillas*, and wrapped around a myriad of fillings to become *tacos*.

To warm flour or corn tortillas for serving as you would bread, heat the oven to 350 F. Wrap the stacked tortillas in aluminum foil and heat for 15 minutes. Bring to the table still wrapped in foil, or transfer to a cloth napkin and place in a basket for serving.

If 15 minutes is too long to wait, and especially if you are eating alone, there is a quicker method for warming. Place the tortillas, one at a time, directly on a gas burner with a low flame. Cook about 45 seconds per side, using tongs to turn, until lightly charred in spots. Tortillas heated this way will stay soft only about 10 minutes, so if you are cooking for more than two, it makes sense to heat the oven instead.

Older, drier tortillas are the best for frying. You can dry them by letting them sit for 30 minutes, uncovered, on a counter before frying. *To crisp-fry tortillas* for chips, strips, and tostadas, pour vegetable or corn oil into a small skillet to a depth of ½ inch. Place over medium heat about 4 minutes, or until bubbles form instantly when a small piece of tortilla is added to the pan. Fry chips by the handful, or one tortilla at a time for tostadas, until golden and puffy, about 45 seconds per side. Drain on paper towels. (You can add salt, if you wish, although you may not find it necessary. Freshly fried tortillas are very tasty.) Fried chips can be reserved in paper bags for a day.

Here is the no-fat method for crisping corn tortillas—not as tasty and rich as the fried kind but good to know for health emergencies: Lay the cut tortillas on a baking sheet and cook in a 350 F oven until lightly brown and crisp, about 15 minutes.

To soften corn tortillas for enchiladas or other wrapped dishes, heat vegetable oil to a depth of ¼ inch in a small skillet over medium-low heat. Cook the tortillas, one at a time, until just soft, about 10 seconds per side. Drain on paper towels and pat dry to absorb any excess oil.

GARNISHES, set on the table for guests to add to taste, are a regular part of Mexican dining. Here are a few ideas that are even quicker than homemade guacamole and salsas: chopped white onions, diced avocado, lime wedges, cilantro sprigs, and quartered and sliced radishes.

COOKING WITH FRESH AND DRIED CHILES. Too much fuss has

A NOTE ABOUT TACOS

☞ IN MEXICO, ANY FOOD THAT CAN BE FOLDED INTO A SOFT CORN TORTILLA AND BROUGHT TO THE MOUTH IS CONSIDERED A TACO. MORE A FAST FOOD THAN A MEAL, TACOS ARE EATEN ON THE RUN AT JUICE BARS, MARKETS, AND STREET STANDS, BUT THEY WOULD NEVER APPEAR ON THE MENU AT A "REAL" RESTAURANT. IN KEEPING WITH THE SPIRIT OF AUTHENTICITY, THERE IS NO RECIPE PER SE FOR TACOS HERE—A FACT MY ELEVEN-YEAR-OLD SON THOROUGHLY DISAPPROVES OF. YET ALL THE FOLLOWING WOULD BE GREAT WRAPPED INSIDE WARM CORN TORTILLAS AND SPRINKLED WITH SOME SALSA, CHOPPED ONIONS, AND CILANTRO: QUESO FUNDIDO (PAGE 35), RAJAS CON CREMA (PAGE 95), CARNITAS (PAGE 70), PORK PICADILLO (PAGE 73), CARNE ASADA (PAGE 76), COCHINITA PIBIL (PAGE 74), BEEF TINGA (PAGE 75), AND SKIRT STEAK WITH ONIONS AND PEPPERS (PAGE 77).

been made about handling hot chile peppers. They are no more complicated to work with than their familiar cousins, bell peppers. I do not recommend wearing gloves because they are too clumsy to work with. I *do* recommend thoroughly washing the knife, cutting surface, and your hands immediately after handling chile peppers to remove any oils or seeds that may have been released from chopping (the veins and seeds are where the heat is stored). Remember, even if there are no seeds visible, the hot oils can easily spread from the knife to other foods or from your hands to your mouth or eyes—so do be careful.

To remove veins and seeds from fresh peppers, make a horizontal cut to remove the stem, then slice in half lengthwise. With a paring knife or the point of a sharp chef's knife, remove the veins and scrape out any remaining seeds. The chile will now be less spicy.

Fresh chile peppers can be roasted using the same method used in Italian cooking for bell peppers. Place on a gas burner over high heat and cook, turning occasionally, until charred all over. Transfer to a plastic bag, tie closed, and set aside to steam about 10 minutes. Rub off the charred skins or scrape carefully with a knife and then remove the seeds and veins as described above.

If your heat source is electric, preheat the broiler and arrange the peppers on a foil-lined baking sheet. Cook, using tongs to turn occasionally, until evenly charred, and then follow the same procedure for sweating and peeling.

Dried chiles need to be softened before they are puréed and added to sauces and stews. If the recipe calls for removing the stems and veins first, simply cut off the stem and tap out the seeds. However, if the pepper is to be roasted first, leave it whole.

To roast dried chiles, first wipe them clean with a damp paper towel. Place a dry cast-iron skillet over medium-low heat and toast the chiles, turning occasionally, until fragrant, from 2 to 5 minutes according to the chile. Then remove the seeds by pulling off the stems and shaking out the seeds. Some recipes, such as moles, may call for toasting the seeds separately, so read the recipe before discarding.

To soften chiles, bring a large kettle of water to a boil. Place the chiles in a large bowl or roasting pan and pour in enough of the hot water to cover generously. Let soak 20 minutes. Read the recipe before discarding the soaking water, as it is often used to thin the puréed chiles.

Mexican Cooking for Beginners

How to Shop for Mexican Cooking

Since the Mexican home pantry is built upon very few ingredients, it is entirely possible to cook good Mexican meals with the ingredients available at your local supermarket or produce store, especially if your market stocks tomatillos, corn tortillas, and two or three of the more popular chile peppers. However, if you live anywhere near a large Mexican or South American market, it is well worth a visit to hone your appetite and reenergize your soul.

Mexican markets are not only places to shop for groceries, they are also places to sample some of the best tacos in town, discuss local politics with the man behind the juice counter, and pick up a piñata for your child's next birthday party. Once the eating is out of the way, you can wend your way through stalls specializing in fruits, vegetables, herbs, dairy products, and baked goods. Staples like rice, beans, lentils, dried chile peppers, and spices are all available in bulk. And besides the fresh tortillas and masa for making tamales that you would expect to find at a Mexican market, you may be lucky enough to find the crusty plain rolls called *bolillos* that are so good for sandwich-making and a treat for breakfast.

The Mexican butcher counter, or *carniceria,* is an excellent source for hard-to-find cuts of meat: tripe, chicken feet, pigs' and lambs' heads, calves' feet, and tongue are all an integral part of Mexican cooking. Butchers also keep succulent cuts of pork and beef marinating in citrus juices, herbs, and spices for quick summer barbecues of tacos from the grill.

INGREDIENTS

Note: An asterisk preceding an ingredient indicates an item recommended for daily cooking.

GRAINS AND LEGUMES

*TORTILLAS are as essential to the Mexican kitchen as pasta is to the Italian. Thin white flour tortillas are favored in the northern states and thicker, more rustic corn tortillas are favored elsewhere. Corn tortillas are the ones to stock if you plan on cooking Mexican food regularly, since they are used in so many other dishes: chilaquiles, tacos, tostadas, huevos rancheros, and enchiladas, to name a few. Flour tortillas, now available with and without lard, are used for making fajitas, burritos, and quesadillas. California supermarkets stock several brands of each, in several sizes, and in quantities ranging from one to five dozen. They are extremely inexpensive and keep well in the refrigerator, in a sealed plastic bag, for about a week.

MASA HARINA, or finely ground corn flour, manufactured by the Quaker Oats Company, is sold in ethnic markets as well as in the baking section of well-stocked supermarkets. It can be used to make homemade tortillas (page 90) or other cornmeal snacks such as gorditas or sopes, but is not suitable for tamales, for which you need to purchase fresh masa specifically prepared for that purpose and stocked by tortilla factories and specialty suppliers. Do not substitute ordinary cornmeal as it is not the same thing. Masa harina is actually corn dough (masa) that has been dried and then ground into a fine flour. It may be stored in a cool, dry place for about a year.

*LONG-GRAIN RICE is the rice used in Mexican cooking. Purchase whatever brand you like and store it in a cool, dry place.

*BEANS. The two most popular beans in the Mexican kitchen are the mottled pink pinto and the small, flavorful black bean. In general, black beans are eaten in the south and pintos in the central and northern states. Pintos are what show up in most Mexican restaurants here in the States. I store 5-pound bags of both in my pantry, where they will keep a good long time. For quick meals I also recommend keeping cans of refried beans on hand. They are not at all bad since they contain only beans, lard, and salt—there are no additives. Canned refried pintos are stocked by many supermarkets, but for refried black beans you may need to visit an ethnic market.

OILS AND VINEGARS

*VEGETABLE AND SAFFLOWER OIL are the two basic oils used in Mexican cooking. Although lard is the traditional cooking fat, I do without it and do not notice any lack of flavor. Vegetable oil will do fine for most dishes. Safflower oil has a subtler flavor and is good for salad dressings or more delicate cooking, and olive oil is good in a few of the Spanish-style dishes, such as Shrimp with Toasted Garlic Sauce (page 79). To add a hint of richness in dishes such as Refried Beans or Cochinita Pibil where lard would ordinarily be used, you can substitute half butter for the oil specified in the recipe.

*APPLE CIDER VINEGAR is a good substitute for the mild pineapple vinegar ordinarily used in Mexican cooking. It is available at the supermarket. **RED WINE VINEGAR** is the other vinegar to keep on hand for salad dressings and sweet-and-sour dishes such as picadillos. Both can be stored in a cupboard indefinitely.

HERBS, SPICES, AND FLAVORINGS

*GARLIC is used to flavor a wide variety of Mexican foods. Except in a few dishes of Spanish origin, it is always used with a light hand—one or two cloves for a serving of four or six will usually suffice. For some dishes, such as roasted salsas, the cloves are first charred to moderate their bitterness. Store large, hard heads of garlic in a cool, dry place.

*CILANTRO, also known as Chinese parsley or fresh coriander, was introduced to Mexico by the Spanish and from there spread north to the American Southwest and south to Latin America. It is indispensable to Mexican cooking, where it is primarily used fresh, as a garnish, and in salsas. It is occasionally puréed and cooked, along with other herbs, into green moles, warm sauces, and rice. Although it is a favorite of Mexican cooks, it is always used with discretion.

Cilantro, which resembles Italian parsley but is thinner, can always be identified by its distinctive aroma. There is nothing else like it. This relatively inexpensive herb is stocked by most supermarkets, and can be stored in the vegetable bin of the refrigerator, in a plastic bag, for about a week, depending on freshness. If the roots are still attached, leave them on, as the herb will last longer. Since cilantro stems are so thin and digestible, you needn't entirely remove them, just trim the bottoms before chopping. Unless you want a purée, always chop cilantro by hand, not in the food processor or blender, as its fragile leaves disintegrate quickly.

*OREGANO is most frequently used in its dried form in the Mexican kitchen, although the fresh herb is a nice addition to homemade marinades. There are two types of dried oregano: Mediterranean and Mexican. Either one will do, although the Mexican has a slightly stronger, more vegetal flavor. It is packaged with leaves and stems in large pieces, so crumble it in the palms of your hands before adding it to the pot.

EPAZOTE is one of those mystery ingredients that cookbook writers say you cannot live without and yet are impossible to find. I have looked everywhere for it, including Los Angeles's ethnic Grand Central market and plant nurseries, to no avail. It is said to be a key ingredient for making southern-style black beans and quesadillas, but you may need to content yourself, as I do, with cooking good Mexican food without it. Although the tastes are dissimilar, I substitute fresh oregano, parsley, or mint for it.

MARJORAM AND ITALIAN PARSLEY are used with some frequency in the Mexican kitchen. Both are easily available at supermarkets and will keep in the vegetable bin of the refrigerator for about a week.

.   .   .   .

In addition to the spices discussed in detail below, the following spices, all available at the supermarket, are used with some regularity in the Mexican kitchen: bay leaf, aniseed, allspice, and clove. Salt is another important seasoning for balancing the flavor of hot chiles.

Dried chile powder should be on hand for times when you can't possibly cope with toasting, soaking, and grinding dried chiles. Make sure you purchase pure chile powder rather than bottled "chili seasoning," which is a combination of ground chile powder, cumin, salt, and other flavorings meant for cooking American-style chili. Use dried chile powder with discretion and always in combination with other spices.

*ANNATTO OR ACHIOTE SEEDS are the small dark red seeds from the South American annatto tree. They are available in some supermarkets that carry ethnic spices and at Mexican and South American markets. When the seeds are ground and combined with other spices and herbs such as garlic, oregano, cumin, cinnamon, pepper, and cloves, they become the *recados*, or seasoning pastes, of the Yucatan. Foods marinated and cooked in such pastes take on an orange color from the annatto and develop a sweet, spicy fragrance similar to tandoor Indian food.

The seeds are a bit difficult to work with because they are so hard. An electric mini-chopper or spice or coffee grinder is perfect for the job, but work in small batches or even those machines will be inefficient. Make sure you wash off any utensils and cutting boards that come in contact with the ground powder quickly, since it is such a powerful dye.

Some ethnic markets sell **ACHIOTE PASTE,** which I recommend instead of grinding the seeds to make your own recados from scratch. These moist orange pastes contain all the ground spices and flavorings and just need to be diluted with vinegar and/or citrus juice. They are much easier to work with and just as authentic. The seeds may be stored in a sealed container in a dry pantry indefinitely, and the paste should be stored, wrapped in plastic, in the refrigerator.

*CINNAMON is used subtly in the Mexican kitchen to flavor both savories and sweets. It adds a hit of sweetness to tomato sauces, moles, and recados—the achiote-based seasoning pastes. The type favored in Mexico and sold in ethnic markets is the soft, flaky kind from Sri Lanka.

*CUMIN is probably the flavor that most conjures up Mexican food for the rest of the world. Unfortunately, the spice is often misunderstood and used too aggressively outside Mexico. Mexican chefs use the seeds of this annual plant sparingly, and always in combination with other flavorings —dried chile peppers, dried coriander, black pepper, and cloves.

*MEXICAN CHOCOLATE is a combination of chocolate, granulated sugar, cinnamon, and ground almonds pressed into disks. It is used to make hot chocolate and the traditional mole poblano. It is not an eating chocolate. Ibarra, the brand most frequently found in the United States, is stocked in Latin American markets. Store the chocolate in a cool, dry place, where it will keep for a year or two.

*SPANISH OLIVES are called for in some casseroles, braised dishes, and seviches. Purchase the small green pitted olives called *manzanillas* or Spanish olives stuffed with pimientos. Both are available at supermarkets and should be stored in their jars in the refrigerator once opened.

DAIRY PRODUCTS

CREMA, or Mexican cream, is used with a light hand as a topping for corn tortilla dishes such as enchiladas and tostadas. It is slightly thicker than heavy cream, with a tart flavor similar to crème fraîche. It is available in bottles in the dairy section of supermarkets where large Latin populations live, or at ethnic markets. Sour cream or plain yogurt are acceptable substitutes.

The cheeses described below are distributed by Mexican food companies to many supermarkets on the West Coast. If they are unavailable in your part of the country, Monterey Jack, mozzarella, white Cheddar cheese, or feta will do fine in most recipes.

*AÑEJO, also known as **COTIJA,** is the sharp, crumbly, dry white cheese that is sprinkled over tostadas and enchiladas. Wrapped well in plastic, it will keep in the refrigerator up to two months. The easiest way to crumble it is to first cut it into thin slices and then chop it roughly. Greek feta and Italian ricotta salata make good substitutes.

PANELA is a moist, slightly sweet white cheese similar in appearance to mozzarella. My favorite Mexican cheese, it is delicious eaten out of the hand with a fresh pear or folded into a corn tortilla and slightly melted on the griddle. String cheese or fresh mozzarella are suitable substitutes.

MANCHEGO is a Spanish-style pale yellow cheese with a salty, nutty flavor similar to provolone. It is an excellent melter and is the traditional choice for queso fundido and quesadillas in southern-central Mexico. Provolone or a mild Parmesan may be substituted.

RANCHERO is a *fresco*, or fresh cheese, and is sometimes labeled as such. It is a soft, sweet, slightly granular cheese that can be crumbled as a garnish or melted. It is also eaten out of the hand as an appetizer in Mexico. Añejo or cotija may be used in its place as a garnish, and Monterey Jack or Cheddar may be substituted for melting.

FRUITS

*LIMES are ubiquitous in the Mexican kitchen. Their tart juice is used as a seasoning in soups and stews and is sprinkled over grilled beef, pork, and seafood, as well as antojitos. Lime is stirred into salsas, rubbed onto margarita glasses, squirted into glasses of cold beer, and licked off the back of the hand before downing a shot of tequila. Small wedges are placed on the table to enliven every meal, including breakfast.

The lime commonly fond in Mexico and called *limone* is closer to the small, thin-skinned key lime than the Persian type sold in our supermarkets. Purchase bright green, firm limes and store in a fruit bowl or basket at room temperature. They give less juice than lemons, so purchase more than you think you will need. As a rule, 1 large lime yields 2 tablespoons fresh juice. Lemon juice is commonly substituted when limes are unavailable, although the flavor is quite different.

*AVOCADOS are used almost as a condiment in the Mexican kitchen. Their rich, mellow flavor and smooth consistency strike a soothing balance with spicy foods. The medium-sized pebbly-skinned Hass, native to Mexico and grown in California, is the first choice for Mexican cooking, if it is available in your region.

An avocado that is not yet ripe is not usable. Ripe avocados have dark green to black skins and feel soft inside when pressed with a thumb. On the other hand, if you can hear the pit rattle when you shake the fruit, it is overripe—the flesh is too soft and beginning to darken. Avocados take 3 to 5 days to ripen at room temperature. Store leftover avocado or guacamole with the pit to retard browning.

PLANTAINS are the wide, thick-skinned bananas used in the Mexican kitchen as a popular side dish along with rice and beans. They are sold in Latin American markets and are not considered ready for cooking until the skin is almost entirely black.

*TOMATOES are as popular in the Mexican kitchen as they are in the Italian. There is some dispute about whether they are native to Peru or Mexico, but they are undoubtedly a New World food brought to the rest of the world's attention by the Spanish. Keep fresh tomatoes ripening in a basket or bowl at room temperature, as you would other fruit, for cooking salsas, soups, stews, and seviches. The whole fruit, including seeds and skin, is often called for in Mexican cooking, so check the recipe before beginning. Canned, peeled, Italian plum tomatoes are always a good substitute in cooked dishes.

BANANA LEAVES are sold in the vegetable section of Latin American markets. Foods that are wrapped in them and then steamed or slow-baked develop a lovely sweet, subtle fragrance. Look for green, pliable leaves, without too many dark spots. Store in a plastic bag in the vegetable

bin of the refrigerator as long as a couple of weeks. If the leaves need to be softened before using, pass them over a gas flame briefly.

VEGETABLES

Fresh vegetables are an integral part of the Mexican diet. In addition to those noted below, potatoes, mushrooms, carrots, lettuce, radishes, broccoli, cauliflower, chayote, and many other kinds of squash and their flowers are either cooked into soups, stews, and casseroles, or served as delicious accompaniments. A friend from Mexico City tells me that a good way to spot a real Mexican restaurant here in the States is by the vegetables. If they are fresh and tasty, chances are the rest of the cooking is authentic as well.

CORN. Since ancient times corn has been Mexico's symbol of sustenance. The Indian word for corn means "our mother" or "life" itself.

Maiz, or dried field corn, is the foundation for masa, the dough for making tortillas, tamales, and the traditional beverages called *atoles*. The whole kernels are used to make hominy for stews and pozoles. The silk makes medicinal teas, and dried husks make wrappers for tamales. (Corn husks, *hojas de maiz* in Spanish, are available in ethnic markets and some supermarkets in the produce section.)

Fresh corn is cooked into soups, stews, and luscious green corn tamales, as well as simply grilled and sold as a street food. One of corn's more exotic by-products—*huitlacoche* (corn fungus or smut)—is now gathering recognition in the rest of the world as a delicacy. Mexican chefs have always used it in soups, crepes, and elegant sauces to add a depth of flavor comparable to truffles. Corn, in short, continues to be everywhere.

HOMINY, a key ingredient in pozole and menudo, is whole kernels of dried white field corn cooked with powdered lime until their skins fall off. After lengthy cooking, the eyes are removed from one end and the kernel blossoms like a flower. Although it is possible to make hominy from scratch, starting with dried field corn and slaked lime, it is extremely time-consuming. I recommend the canned product called white or Mexican-style hominy that is sold in most supermarkets.

*ONIONS, along with tomatoes and chiles, are one of the dominant flavorings of Mexican food. Unless otherwise specified, the more piquant white onions, rather than yellow, are always first choice for Mexican cooking. Grilled scallions often show up as a garnish with other grilled foods, and red onions provide a nice contrast for salads and are a common garnish in Yucatecan cooking. Store onions in a cool, dry place.

*TOMATILLOS, also known as Mexican green tomatoes, are the small, round green fruits sold in papery husks that are the basis for most green sauces and moles. They are not really related to the tomato but are part of the cherry family. Their sharp, acidic flavor is often toned down by first parboiling or roasting. Before cooking, always remove the husks by hand and rinse the fruit. Tomatillos are stocked by most supermarkets. They should be stored in a bag in the vegetable bin of the refrigerator, where they will keep as long as two weeks, depending on freshness.

JICAMA is a large brown-skinned tuber whose pink-white firm, moist flesh is a refreshing addition to salads and quick-cooked dishes. In Mexico, it is peeled, sliced, then dipped in lime juice and sprinkled with chile powder, and eaten out of hand almost as a fruit. Jicama, which is also used in Asian cooking, is stocked by most supermarkets. Store in the vegetable bin of the refrigerator, wrapped in plastic, and peel as needed.

*CHILE PEPPERS, both fresh and dried, are the primary source of the heat for which Mexican food is so famous. Although you cannot do without them, you can get along very well with the six or so varieties that are currently available in the supermarket.

As a general rule, larger chiles tend to be sweeter and milder than smaller ones. Just remember: The heat, or capsaicin, is contained in the placenta, or sack of seeds and veins located under the stem. If you remove them, the chile will be less hot. The other thing to remember is that tortillas, rice, beans, dairy, sugar, and salt are the time-honored antidotes to a chile-seared mouth. Other than that, time heals all wounds.

Chile peppers are classified botanically as fruits. They are believed to have originated in Bolivia in the eighth century B.C., when the seeds were distributed by birds throughout Central and South America. They were revered by the Aztecs and Mayans and were brought back to Spain by Columbus. From there they spread rapidly throughout Europe and found an appreciative audience in Asia and India.

There are hundreds of types of chiles in the world today. Even within Mexico, the same chile may go by a different name in different regions and may taste quite different from region to region, due to the soil or climate. Chiles grown during the hot summer months, for instance, will be hotter than those harvested in the winter. For the purposes of this book, I have called for only chiles that are widely available and whose tastes and characteristics are fairly consistent in American markets.

Fresh chiles—serranos, jalapeños, poblanos, Anaheims—can be stored in plastic bags in the vegetable bin of the refrigerator about a week, or until they start softening. When shopping, look for the same things you look for in a bell pepper: smooth, unblemished skins and fruit that feels firm when pressed.

Serrano chiles are the smallest and hottest of the fresh chiles commonly found at the market. They are popular in Thai and Indian cooking and are an important ingredient in salsa making. These bright green chiles are about 2 inches long, quite narrow, and very hot.

Jalapeño chiles rode the recent wave of Cajun and southwestern cooking to become the best known in this country. In Mexico they are used in salsas, seviches, casseroles, and stews, and they are also pickled and served as a condiment. These small chile peppers are a bit wider and longer than the serrano and are less hot. Jalapeños and serranos may be used interchangeably where both are not available. Just use fewer serranos to jalapeños, or use the seeds accordingly.

Poblano chiles, sometimes mislabeled pasillas, are dark green, medium-size peppers with a triangular shape. They are about 6 inches long and 3 inches wide at the stem end. Their hot, meaty flesh make them an excellent choice for chiles rellenos and rajas (roasted pepper strips). Since they can be quite hot, most recipes call for roasting and then removing the seeds and veins.

Anaheim chiles were popular for chiles rellenos before American tastebuds became accustomed to the hotter poblanos. These long, thin pale-green chiles are quite mild, though they are still favored by some for stuffing and for making stews. The fire-roasted canned product by Ortega is quite good for quesadillas or other quick-cooked foods, although not sturdy enough for stuffing.

Dried chiles as a rule are more complex in character than fresh chiles. They add a smoky, sweet quality as well as heat to dishes in which they are cooked. The more common dried chiles—de arbol, California, and New Mexico—can be found in the produce section of some supermarkets. For a wider selection, you may need to visit an ethnic market. When shopping, look for unbroken chiles that are still flexible. Always wipe them off with a damp paper towel before toasting or soaking. Store in plastic bags in a cool, dry place, where they will keep indefinitely.

Chiles de arbol are small, thin, orange-red chiles with smooth but brittle skin. These extremely volatile little chiles are used in salsas and in Chinese Szechuan-style dishes.

Ancho chiles are medium-size, dark red, wrinkled chiles with a distinctive prune fragrance. The dried form of the poblano, they are commonly toasted, soaked, and puréed into salsas and moles, where they add mild heat along with a sweet, fruity flavor.

Pasilla chiles are so similar in appearance to anchos that it can be difficult to tell them apart. They are about 5 inches long and nearly black in color. These complex medium-hot chiles are usually toasted before being crumbled into soups, like Tortilla soup, or puréed into rustic table sauces and moles. Where both are not available, pasilla and ancho chiles may be used interchangeably.

California or New Mexico chiles are the dried form of the long, green Anaheim chile. They are long and thin with smooth, flexible, deep red skin. Their flavor is more sweet than hot and can be quite one-dimensional if not blended with other chile flavors. They are the basis for red enchilada sauces, as well as other sauces and stews.

Chipotle chiles en adobo are dried, smoked jalapeños pickled in an adobo sauce of tomatoes, vinegar, and seasonings. They add a complex sweet, smoky, and spicy flavor to marinades and sauces and have become quite popular in southwestern foods. They are available in cans at Latin American markets. Once opened, transfer the contents to a plastic container, which can be stored in the refrigerator up to two weeks.

NUTS AND SEEDS

Nuts and seeds have played an important role in the cooking of Mexico since pre-Columbian times. Peanuts, pecans, and pumpkin seeds (pepitas) were all in use before the Spaniards arrived. And walnuts, almonds, and sesame seeds were adopted during the colonial period.

Today nuts and seeds are called for in a wide variety of both savory and sweet dishes. They are ground together to form a whole category of nut- and seed-based sauces called *pipians*, and they are used to thicken moles and pozoles. Almonds are the main ingredient in almendrado sauces for poultry; walnuts the main ingredient in the sauce for the national dish, chiles en nogado, and peanuts are delectable in the rich, red cacahuate sauce for chicken. A favorite Mexican snack, often eaten at the start of a meal, is roasted, salted, chile-seasoned peanuts or pumpkin seeds.

I recommend purchasing plain, unroasted nuts and seeds in health food stores, where the supply is fresh. They can all be stored, in plastic bags or containers, in the freezer for up to six months. Nuts and seeds need not be defrosted before using.

EQUIPMENT FOR THE MEXICAN KITCHEN

The Mexican kitchen is comfortably low-tech. I was able to test all the recipes for the this book with the equipment on hand in my home kitchen except for one inexpensive cast-iron tortilla press. You will be well prepared if you have the following:

Heavy, black cast-iron skillets for roasting, toasting, and frying. I like to use an 8-inch one for small quantities of seeds and spices and for frying tortillas in a minimum of oil, and a 10- or 12-inch skillet for just about everything else. Cast iron is inexpensive, easy to season, and comes closest to the equipment used in Mexico. In Mexican homes, *comals* (griddles made of steel or cast iron) are kept on the stove top all day long for all the roasting and toasting tasks. Although I wouldn't rush out and buy one, a griddle or comal will make homemade tortilla making a bit easier.

Electrical equipment for grinding and puréeing. A blender is a necessity

for puréeing small quantities for salsas and rice and for making a number of traditional drinks, including margaritas. A food processor, though it may not liquefy to quite as fine a consistency as a blender, is the most practical choice for puréeing larger quantities for salsas, soups, and moles and for grinding nuts. And an electric mini-chopper or coffee grinder is perfect for grinding hard, whole seeds like annatto and whole spices.

All of this modern equipment takes the place of the traditional three-legged lava stone bowl and pestle, called the *molcajete,* and the *metate,* or flat grinding stone. Although they are picturesque and can be purchased at ethnic markets, think of them mainly in terms of display. Even in Mexico the blender has become commonplace.

A large enameled cast-iron dutch oven with lid for braising foods and cooking beans. Although the traditional material in Mexico for cooking pots is clay, which has been low-fired and glazed on the inside, it seems impractical when such good, sturdy kitchenware is available. On the other hand, painted clay pots also look beautiful on the display shelf.

The only other piece of equipment that comes in handy, especially if you are timid about roasting directly on the flame, is the portable grate that fits over the burner sold in kitchenware and department stores. I use it for heating tortillas and making the fat-free Quesadillas on page 36. It is fun but definitely not a necessity.

SOUPS

THE MEXICAN APPETITE FOR SOUP IS SO LARGE IT TAKES THREE WORDS TO DESCRIBE IT. FIRST THERE ARE THE *SOPAS*, OR FLAVORFUL BROTHS SUCH AS TORTILLA SOUP, THAT USUALLY BEGIN A LARGER, MULTICOURSE MEAL. THEN THERE ARE THE *CALDOS*, OR HEARTIER BROTHS SUCH AS MEXICAN FISH SOUP (PAGE 30), THAT ARE SUBSTANTIAL AND INTERESTING ENOUGH TO SERVE AS ENTRÉES. AND FINALLY THERE ARE THE RIB-STICKING *POZOLES* AND *MENUDOS,* MORE STEWS THAN SOUPS—SO THICK AND RICH THEY ARE TOTALLY UNLIKE ANYTHING IN EUROPEAN CUISINE. HERE IS A SMALL SAMPLING OF THE LIGHTER SOPAS, ALONG WITH ONE BEGINNER'S POZOLE AND AN EASY FISH STOCK THAT SERVES AS THE BASIS FOR THE DELICIOUS MAIN-COURSE FISH SOUP.

TORTILLA SOUP

Tortilla soup is as easy to make as it is to love. It is simply chicken stock enriched with the earthy flavors of roasted tomatoes, toasted chiles, and crispy tortilla strips. ✗ *Serves 4*

3 medium tomatoes
1 small white onion, roughly
  chopped
2 garlic cloves, peeled
½ cup vegetable oil
½ teaspoon ground cumin
5 cups chicken broth

1 teaspoon salt
1 dried pasilla pepper, wiped clean
  with a damp paper towel
8 dry corn tortillas
¼ cup chopped fresh cilantro
1 ripe avocado, cut into small
  chunks

1] Preheat the broiler and line a baking sheet with aluminum foil. Put tomatoes on the sheet and place under the broiler, turning frequently with tongs until softened and charred all over. Set aside to cool.

2] In a food processor fitted with the metal blade, or a blender, purée the onion and garlic. Add the tomatoes, with skins and cores. Purée until smooth.

3] In a medium dutch oven or stockpot, heat 1 tablespoon of the vegetable oil over medium-low heat. Pour in the puréed tomato mixture and cumin. Cook at a low boil, stirring occasionally, to intensify the flavors, about 6 minutes. Stir in the chicken broth and salt and bring to a boil. Skim and discard any foam that rises to the top. Reduce to a simmer and cook, uncovered, about 20 minutes.

4] Meanwhile prepare the garnishes: Heat the remaining vegetable oil in a small skillet over medium heat. Briefly cook the pasilla pepper in the oil until shiny, black, and puffy, about 2 minutes. Drain on a paper towel. When cool enough to handle, tear apart, discarding the stem, and crumble the blackened pepper into small pieces. Place along with the seeds in a condiment bowl for serving.

5] Reduce the heat under the pan to medium-low. Trim the tortillas into strips by first cutting into semicircles and then into thin ¼-inch strips. Fry by the handful in the hot oil until golden and crisp, turning occasionally with tongs. Transfer to paper towels to drain.

6] To serve, divide the tortilla strips and place in 4 soup bowls. Ladle on the hot soup and sprinkle with chopped cilantro. Serve with crumbled pasilla pepper and chopped avocado.

VARIATIONS. For a richer soup—more appropriate for a light supper than a first course—poach 2 chicken breast halves in water for 20 minutes. Bone, peel, and dice. Add to the broth along with the garnishes and ½ cup fresh or good quality mozzarella cheese cut into ¼-inch cubes. For an easy version of Yucatecan sopa de lima, add 2 sliced limes to the broth as it begins to simmer, add the diced chicken as above, and then serve with additional lime quarters.

SUMMER CORN SOUP

Always taste a raw kernel before you go to the trouble of making corn soup from scratch. If it doesn't taste sweet, the flavor will not improve with cooking—better to substitute frozen. Substitute half cream for the milk if you prefer a richer soup. ✂ *Serves 4*

4 tablespoons unsalted butter
1 white onion, sliced
1 garlic clove, chopped
2 teaspoons dried oregano
6 ears fresh corn, husks and silk
  removed, kernels scraped off the
  cob, or 4 cups frozen kernels

2 cups chicken broth
2 cups milk
1 teaspoon salt
Crumbled añejo or mild feta
  cheese, for garnish

1] Melt the butter in a dutch oven or stockpot over medium heat. Cook the onions, garlic, and oregano until soft, 5 minutes. Add the corn kernels and cook, stirring frequently to avoid scorching, 8 minutes longer.

2] Transfer the hot corn mixture along with ½ cup of the chicken broth to a food processor fitted with a metal blade. Purée several minutes, until as smooth as possible. Return the purée to the stockpot.

3] Pour in the remaining chicken broth, milk, and salt. Cook, uncovered, over low heat for 15 minutes. Skim and discard any foam from the top. Serve hot with crumbled cheese for sprinkling.

BASIC BLACK BEAN SOUP

━━━━━━━━━ ■ ━━━━━━━━━

This thick, savory soup makes a wonderful winter supper served with warm corn tortillas and perhaps Watercress, Jicama, and Orange Salad (page 43) for contrast. There is nothing complicated about preparing bean soup. The beans do not need to be presoaked, and once they are boiled, which can be done a day or so in advance, the soup can be finished in 15 minutes. You may want to place a bowl of Salsa Fresca (page 47) on the table as an additional garnish for those who want heat with their Mexican food. ✖ *Serves 6*

6 cups cooked black beans in
  their broth (page 88)
4 slices bacon, chopped
1 medium white onion, diced
1 teaspoon ground cumin

1 cup water, or more to taste
Freshly ground pepper
2 tablespoons lime juice
Sour cream and chopped fresh
  cilantro, for garnish

1] Transfer the beans with their cooking liquid, 2 cups at a time, to the bowl of a food processor fitted with a metal blade. Purée until the beans are broken and a chunky purée is formed. Reserve.

2] In a dutch oven or stockpot over moderate heat, fry the bacon, stirring with a wooden spoon to break up the pieces, until the fat is rendered. Reduce the heat to low and add the onion and cumin. Cook, stirring occasionally, until the onion is soft.

3] Pour in the puréed beans and water. Season with black pepper, and salt if necessary. Bring to a boil, reduce to a simmer, and cook 10 minutes. Remove from heat and stir in the lime juice. Garnish each serving with a dollop of sour cream and some cilantro.

JOSEPHINE'S POZOLE

More a stew than a soup, pozole is one of those Mexican dishes that have several regional variations. There is a pungent green version from Guerrero and a chile-laden one from Michoacan, as well as a popular white version from Guadalajara. What they all share is the combination of pork and hominy and long, slow cooking.

This particular version, from friend and caterer Jo Gruendemann, makes no claims to authenticity. What it does promise, however, is ease of preparation and a soul-satisfying fall or winter meal. Serve with a basket of warm flour tortillas. ✖ *Serves 6 to 8*

¼ cup vegetable oil
1 large white onion, diced
4 large garlic cloves, minced
1 to 2 tablespoons dried red chile powder
2 pounds boneless pork loin, cut into 1-inch cubes
2 (15 ounce) cans white hominy
2 quarts water

1 tablespoon plus 1 teaspoon dried oregano
2 teaspoons whole black peppercorns
1½ teaspoons salt
1 large celery rib, diced
1 large carrot, peeled and diced
1 green bell pepper, cored, seeded, and diced

1] Heat the oil in a heavy dutch oven or stockpot over moderate heat. Cook the onion, garlic, and chile powder, stirring frequently, until the onion is soft, about 5 minutes. Add the pork cubes and continue cooking over medium to high heat until the meat is evenly browned, about 10 minutes longer.

2] Stir in the hominy with its liquid, the water, oregano, pepper, and salt. Bring to a boil and skim and discard the foam that rises to the top. Reduce to a simmer and cook, partially covered, 2 hours, or until the meat and hominy kernels are soft but not mushy.

3] Add the remaining diced vegetables and simmer, uncovered, 30 minutes longer. Taste and adjust with salt, chile powder, and pepper. Serve hot with warm flour tortillas.

ALBÓNDIGAS SOUP

Meatballs, or *albóndigas,* often appear as an entrée in a sauce of chiles and nuts as well as in this popular mild-mannered soup.

✖ *Serves 6*

¼ cup milk
1 (1-inch) slice dry white bread, crusts removed
½ pound ground beef
½ pound ground pork
2 large garlic cloves, minced
3 tablespoons ground almonds
1 egg
1½ teaspoons ground cumin
1 teaspoon dried oregano
¾ teaspoon salt
Freshly ground pepper

4 cups chicken broth
2 cups water
1 small white onion, diced
1 medium zucchini, trimmed and cut into ¼-inch cubes
2 carrots, peeled and cut into ¼-inch cubes
1 tomato, peeled, seeded, and diced
Salt to taste
¼ cup chopped fresh cilantro

1] Pour the milk into a small bowl and soak the bread in it until soft.

2] In a large mixing bowl, combine the ground beef, pork, garlic, almonds, egg, cumin, oregano, salt, and pepper. When the bread is soft, break into small pieces and add to the meat. Hands are the best tool for combining these ingredients.

3] Pour the chicken broth and water into a stockpot or large saucepan and bring to a boil.

4] Form meatballs by gently rolling about 2 tablespoons of the meat mixture between your palms to form small balls. Reserve on a plate.

5] Add, one at a time, to the boiling broth along with the onion. Skim and discard the foam that rises to the top. Reduce to a simmer and cook, uncovered, 15 minutes.

6] Add the zucchini, carrots, and tomatoes and return to a boil. Reduce to a simmer and cook another 20 minutes. Taste the broth, add salt as desired, and stir in cilantro. Simmer 5 minutes longer and serve steaming hot.

MEXICAN FISH SOUP

Mexico has a rich tradition of wonderful hearty soups called *caldos,* which are thick and satisfying enough to be eaten as the main part of the meal. Similar to a Mediterranean bouillabaisse, this full-flavored fish soup is a good choice for cool-weather entertaining with perhaps a salad and some crusty baguettes. Any flaky white fish such as red snapper may be substituted for the bass or flounder.

✖ *Serves 4 as an entrée, 6 as an appetizer*

3 tablespoons olive oil
1 medium white onion, diced
3 garlic cloves, minced
1 teaspoon salt
2 medium tomatoes, peeled, seeded, and diced (page 81)
4 cups fish stock (recipe follows), or 2 cups bottled clam juice mixed with 2 cups water
3 small boiling potatoes, unpeeled, cut into chunks
1 ear fresh corn, cleaned and cut across the width into ½-inch slices

1 teaspoon dried oregano
1 pound sea bass fillets, cut into 2-inch chunks
1 pound flounder fillets, cut into 2-inch chunks
½ pound large shrimp, peeled and deveined
Salt, freshly ground pepper, and Tabasco to taste
Juice of ½ lime
1 jalapeño pepper, seeded, deveined, and minced
½ cup fresh cilantro leaves
Lime wedges, for garnishes

1] In a large nonaluminum stockpot or dutch oven, heat the oil over medium-high heat. Sauté the onion and garlic with salt until golden, about 4 minutes. Add the tomato and continue cooking, stirring frequently, another 5 minutes.

2] Pour in the fish stock and add the potatoes, corn, and oregano. Bring to a boil, reduce to a simmer, and cook, uncovered, 20 minutes.

3] Add the sea bass and flounder. Bring to a boil, reduce to a simmer, and cook, covered, 10 minutes, or until the fish is opaque. Add the shrimp. Bring back to a simmer and cook, covered, 2 minutes longer. Season with salt, pepper, Tabasco, and lime juice. Serve hot with small bowls of jalapeño pepper, cilantro, and lime wedges for guests to season at the table.

FISH STOCK

You can purchase fish heads and bones from a busy fish store. My local store seals them in plastic bags and keeps them in the freezer for potential stock makers. Unlike poultry and meat stock, fish stock does suffer from overcooking, so do follow the timing in the recipe. It is also quite perishable, so don't store it too long. ✖ *Makes 6 cups*

2 tablespoons olive oil
1 carrot, peeled and chopped
1 celery rib, chopped
1 onion, chopped
2 garlic cloves, chopped
2 pounds fish bones and heads

7 cups water
1 cup dry white wine
4 bay leaves
1 teaspoon black peppercorns
4 parsley sprigs
½ teaspoon dried thyme

1] In a large stockpot or dutch oven (not aluminum), heat the oil over medium-high heat. Sauté the carrot, celery, onion, and garlic until golden. Add the bones and sauté 5 minutes longer, stirring frequently.

2] Pour in the water and wine and add the remaining ingredients. Bring to a boil, reduce to a simmer, and skim and discard the foam that rises to the top. Cook, uncovered, 40 minutes. Strain the broth, discarding the solids, and set aside to cool. Fish broth can be stored in a sealed container in the refrigerator for 3 to 4 days, or frozen up to a month. Remove the layer of fat from the top before using.

APPETIZERS AND SALADS

In Mexico, appetizers such as the ones described in this chapter are more likely to be eaten during the day as snacks or small meals than as dinner appetizers. They have been brought together here with the idea that they can be served either in small portions as starters or in larger portions as small meals. Here are a few of my favorite corn tortilla—based snacks known as *antojitos*, or little whims, along with recipes for watercress salad, a couple of refreshing fish salads, guacamole, and that all-time favorite from Tijuana, Caesar salad.

QUESO FUNDIDO

This cozy little dish, also known as *queso flameado* in parts of Mexico, is traditionally served in rustic earthenware crocks called *cazuelitas*. The classic topping is chorizo sausage and chile strips, but there are many vegetable variations such as the one given here. Warm tortillas are perfect for scooping up the cheese. ✻ *Serves 4*

2 cups (½ pound) shredded
  Monterey jack, manchego, or
  mozzarella cheese
1 cup crumbled feta cheese or
  queso añejo

1 tablespoon butter
1 medium zucchini, trimmed and
  diced
10 mushroom caps, thinly sliced
Freshly ground pepper

1] Preheat the oven to 375 F.

2] Combine the cheeses. Divide and place in 4 ovenproof ½-cup ramekins or one 9-inch square ovenproof baking dish. (Do not be concerned if they are almost overflowing; the heat will melt the cheese down.) Place on a baking tray or cookie sheet for easy handling and bake for 5 minutes, until the cheese begins to soften.

3] Meanwhile, melt the butter in a small skillet over medium-high heat. Sauté the zucchini and mushrooms with a sprinkling of black pepper until lightly browned, about 5 minutes.

4] Sprinkle the zucchini and mushrooms over the cheese and place back in the oven about 7 minutes longer, until the cheese is melted and bubbly. Use tongs or pot holders to transfer the dishes to individual serving plates and serve immediately with soft, warm tortillas.

QUESADILLAS

Traditional quesadillas consist of an uncooked round of corn masa wrapped around some herb-seasoned cheese, which is then lightly toasted on the *comal*. The result is doughier and more like an empanada or turnover than the version we are familiar with. This recipe is for the type typically served in Mexican restaurants in the States.

Serves 4

2 teaspoons vegetable oil
4 regular-size flour tortillas
1½ cups (10 ounces) grated Monterey Jack cheese

2 (canned) whole green fire-roasted chiles, diced
1 ripe medium tomato, cored and diced

1] Preheat the oven to 200 F. Have ready a baking tray or cookie sheet.

2] Heat the vegetable oil in a heavy 10-inch skillet over medium-high heat. Place a tortilla in the pan and cook a few seconds to heat through. Sprinkle with about 6 tablespoons of cheese to within ½ inch of the outside edge. Divide the chiles and tomatoes into 4 portions. Scatter first the chiles and then the tomatoes over the cheese. When the cheese begins to melt, fold the tortilla in half with a spatula. Tamp down the edges to enclose the filling and cook until the bottom is golden, about 30 seconds. Turn over and cook the other side until golden. (You want to stop cooking just before the cheese oozes out.) Transfer to the baking tray and keep warm in the oven. Repeat with the remaining tortillas. Cut each into 3 wedges and serve hot.

VARIATIONS. Quesadillas are the pizza of Mexican food. There are limitless variations. For a more authentic flavor try a salty Mexican melting cheese like ranchero or a panela with lightly sautéed zucchini blossoms. Or go cross-cultural with uptown fillings like Brie and papaya. The children of the house, on the other hand, can be kept quite happy with your basic shredded Jack or Cheddar cheeses—without the chile peppers.

A Quesadilla Alternative

☞ HERE IS A QUICK GREASE-FREE METHOD FOR MAKING QUESADILLAS RIGHT ON THE STOVE TOP OR ON ONE OF THOSE CROSS-HATCHED GRATES THAT CAN BE PLACED DIRECTLY OVER THE BURNER. (YOU DO NEED A GAS RANGE AND COOKING TONGS TO USE THIS METHOD.) TURN THE HEAT ON LOW AND PLACE A CORN TORTILLA DIRECTLY ON THE BURNER. LET IT COOK FOR A MINUTE OR TWO, JUST UNTIL SLIGHTLY CRISP, AND THEN TURN WITH A PAIR OF TONGS. PLACE SOME THINLY SLICED CHEESE (I LIKE PANELA FOR THIS) ON HALF THE TORTILLA AND FOLD IN HALF TO ENCLOSE. CONTINUE COOKING OVER A LOW FLAME, TURNING THE TORTILLA NOW AND THEN UNTIL IT IS CHARRED IN SPOTS AND THE CHEESE IS SOFT. THREE OF THESE MAKE A WONDERFUL SMALL LUNCH.

NACHOS WITH BLACK BEANS

In Mexico, nachos do not mean corn chips floating in fluorescent orange glop. They are a high-protein snack of crisp-fried corn tortillas topped with cheese and sausage, beef and salsa, or refried black beans and pungent añejo cheese. ✕ *Serves 4*

4 corn tortillas
1 cup Refried Beans (page 89)
Vegetable oil, for frying

½ cup crumbled cotija, añejo, or mild feta cheese

1] Set the tortillas out on a counter to dry. Reheat the black beans over low heat, using a bit of chicken broth if necessary to thin. Preheat the broiler.

2] In a small (8-inch) skillet, heat ½ inch of vegetable oil to 380 F on a deep-fat thermometer. Line the counters with paper towels. Fry 1 tortilla at a time until golden brown and crisp on both sides, about 1½ minutes total. Transfer to paper towels to drain.

3] Arrange the fried tortillas on a baking sheet. Spread ¼ cup of black beans over each, leaving ½ inch bare around the rims. Sprinkle each with 2 tablespoons of cheese. Place under the broiler just until the cheese softens, less than a minute. Be careful not to burn the tortilla edges. Transfer to serving plates, cut into quarters, and serve. You can dress up this simple presentation by serving nachos over a bed of shredded iceberg lettuce.

VARIATION. Just about any good melting cheese can be grated and used for nachos. Besides the ubiquitous Cheddar or Jack cheeses, mozzarella, fontina, Gruyère, and Muenster all melt well. Fry the tortillas as in the recipe above and quickly melt the cheese under the broiler.

GUACAMOLE

There are as many variations of this popular table condiment as there are cooks in Mexico. This version emphasizes the rich flavor of avocado by omitting the tomato. Omit the jalapeño seeds also, if you prefer your guacamole milder. Guacamole is the all-purpose topping for quesadillas, tacos, carnitas, and, of course, fried corn chips. It also makes a great spread for sandwiches of turkey, chicken, or pork.

✖ *Makes 2 cups, or 6 appetizer portions*

3 ripe, medium avocados,
  preferably Hass
1 jalapeño pepper, with seeds
½ white onion, finely minced
3 tablespoons finely chopped
  cilantro

1 tablespoon lime juice
¼ teaspoon salt
3 dashes of Tabasco

1] Cut the avocados in half lengthwise and twist apart. Remove the seeds and scoop out pulp by running a tablespoon between skin and meat or, if ripe enough, gently squeeze to remove skin. Roughly chop and place in a bowl.

2] Add the remaining ingredients and gently mix and toss with a fork so that chunks of avocado remain visible. If you prefer a smoother purée, just stir and mash more vigorously. Taste and adjust seasonings with salt, Tabasco, and lime juice. Store, covered with plastic wrap, in the refrigerator with an avocado pit tucked in the center to retain the color. Guacamole should not be made more than 2 hours in advance since it fades so quickly.

SEVICHE

Seviche, the raw fish cocktail, is almost as well known here as it is all over Mexico. It is wonderful warm-weather food served on some crisp lettuce leaves or on top of a tostada. Swordfish, scallops, sea bass, sierra, and mackerel are all good substitutes for snapper. ✗ *Serves 6*

¾ pound red snapper fillets
1 cup fresh lime juice (about
    10 limes)
2 large tomatoes, seeded and diced
½ large red onion, finely diced
2 jalapeño or serrano chiles, seeds
    and veins removed, diced
¼ cup olive oil

1 tablespoon red wine vinegar
½ cup tomato juice
1 tablespoon plus 2 teaspoons
    chopped fresh oregano or
    marjoram
½ teaspoon salt
Freshly ground pepper and
    Tabasco

1] Press the fillets to check for bones. There may still be a thin strip of rib bones running in a line—just cut them out in a strip with the tip of a sharp knife. Cut the fish into ½-inch cubes. Place in a shallow glass or ceramic bowl and pour on the lime juice to cover. Cover with plastic wrap and refrigerate 4 to 5 hours, or until the largest piece is opaque in the center.

2] Drain the fish in a strainer or colander, discarding the lime juice.

3] Combine the remaining ingredients in a bowl and toss with the fish. Adjust seasonings with salt, pepper, and Tabasco. Serve or chill until serving time. Seviche may be kept in the refrigerator up to 24 hours.

CRAB TOSTADITOS

This easy version of *salpicón de jaiba*—or medley of shredded crabmeat—is one of my favorites. I love the way the richness of the crab and avocado are offset by the sharpness of onion and olives. It is perfect cocktail party food. The crab salad and dressing can be mixed in advance and the quantities can easily be doubled or tripled for a larger crowd. ✗ *Makes 24 pieces, or 4 appetizer servings*

½ pound cleaned, flaked crabmeat
¼ cup finely chopped green
　Spanish olives stuffed with
　pimientos
½ cup roughly chopped cilantro
　leaves
3 tablespoons minced red onion
1 medium tomato
2 tablespoons red wine vinegar

2 tablespoons fresh lime juice
2 tablespoons mild olive oil
3 or 4 dashes of Tabasco
¼ teaspoon salt
4 corn tortillas, fried for chips
　(page 91)
1 ripe avocado, peeled, thinly
　sliced, and halved
Freshly ground pepper

1] Place the crabmeat in a ceramic or glass bowl. Mix in the olives, cilantro, and onion.

2] Julienne the tomato by first cutting into quarters. Cut out and discard the soft interior pulp and seeds, leaving the flesh that is attached to the skin. Stack the quarters and cut into thin strips, or julienne. Then cut crosswise into dice. Add to the crab salad.

3] In a small bowl, whisk together the red wine vinegar, lime juice, olive oil, Tabasco, and salt. Pour over the crab mixture and mix well. Cover and chill about 4 hours to marry the flavors.

4] Just before serving time, fry the tortilla chips and arrange on serving plates or a platter. Top each with a tablespoon of cold crab mixture. Top with a slice of avocado, sprinkle with black pepper, and serve.

CHICKEN TOSTADAS

In Mexico, tostadas, or crisp-fried tortillas, are served with a wide range of toppings, from shark and seviche along the coasts to stringy beef or shredded chicken in the interior. In the United States, however, tostadas almost always mean chicken, served with mounds of lettuce, beans, and cheese inside a huge deep-fried tortilla basket.

This easy recipe, which calls for crisp-fried tortillas, is much closer to what is eaten in Mexico. It makes a nutritious complete little meal, with its vegetables, beans, chicken, and corn tortilla. If you are in a rush, just substitute a roasted chicken from the take-out counter, remove the skin and bones, and shred the meat. ✖ *Serves 4 as a main course*

4 chicken breast halves, with skin and bone
1 (14.5 ounce) can chicken broth
1 medium head romaine lettuce, washed and dried
2 large tomatoes, cored and cut into small wedges
1 red onion, halved and thinly sliced
2 small or 1 large avocado, cut into chunks

6 tablespoons safflower oil
2 tablespoons red wine vinegar
Salt and freshly ground pepper to taste
1 (16 ounce) can or 2 cups homemade refried beans, pinto, or black beans (page 89)
Safflower oil, for frying
8 corn tortillas
8 ounces añejo or mild feta cheese, crumbled (2 cups)

1] Poach the chicken breasts by placing in a large saucepan. Pour in the chicken broth and enough cold water to just cover the chicken. Bring to a boil, reduce to a simmer, and cook, uncovered, 20 minutes. Transfer the chicken to a platter to cool and save the liquid in the pan.

2] Stack the lettuce leaves, roll in a cylinder, and thinly slice across the width. Place in a bowl, along with tomatoes, red onion, and avocado. Gently toss.

3] Make salad dressing by whisking together the safflower oil and red wine vinegar. Season with salt and pepper. Pour over the salad and toss to combine. If making in advance, reserve the salad and dressing separately in the refrigerator and combine just before serving.

4] Remove and discard the chicken skin and separate the meat from the bones. Shred the chicken or roughly chop into bite-size pieces. If preparing in advance, moisten with a few tablespoons of chicken broth, sprinkle with salt if desired, and cover with plastic wrap until serving time.

5] Just before serving, empty the refried beans into a small saucepan and moisten with a few tablespoons of the reserved chicken broth. Place over low heat, stirring occasionally to avoid scorching, until heated through.

6] Heat ½ inch safflower oil in a small skillet over moderate heat. Fry one tortilla at a time, until golden and crisp, about 45 seconds per side. Drain on paper towels. (This may be done up to 2 hours in advance.)

7] To assemble, place 2 tortillas on each dinner plate. Spread a thin layer of warm beans over each. Scatter on the chicken and then cover with the salad. Sprinkle with cheese and serve.

WATERCRESS, JICAMA, AND ORANGE SALAD

This light and refreshing salad fairly snaps with the crispness of tart watercress leaves and crunchy sweet jicama. It is wonderful either at the beginning or end of a rich, spicy meal. ✕ *Serves 6*

8 cups watercress
1 medium jicama, peeled and cut
  into 2-inch-long matchsticks
  (2 cups)

4 medium oranges
¼ cup safflower oil
Salt and freshly ground pepper

1] Wash, stem, and trim the watercress into about 2-inch lengths and place in a large bowl with the jicama.

2] Peel the oranges and then hold each over the salad bowl and cut on either side of the membranes with a serrated blade to loosen the sections. Add them to the salad along with the juices that drip as you cut.

3] Pour on the oil, sprinkle with salt and pepper, and toss well. Taste and adjust with oil, additional orange juice, or salt and pepper. Serve immediately.

CAESAR SALAD

Caesar salad was invented by Tijuana restaurateur Caesar Cardini on July 4th weekend, 1924. According to John Mariani, in his *Dictionary of American Food and Drink,* the dish was originally served as a main course with whole lettuce leaves, absolutely no anchovies, and two coddled eggs. It immediately caught on with the Hollywood crowd who visited Tijuana and became a mainstay on fashionable Los Angeles restaurant menus—where it is still a bestseller.

The version recorded here is a late twentieth-century one for the home cook. Reduce or omit the anchovies if you wish, and the partially cooked egg if you are squeamish. You can prepare both the leaves and dressing in advance and keep them chilled separately. ✖ *Serves 4*

DRESSING
4 anchovies
2 garlic cloves, crushed and peeled
⅓ cup olive oil
¼ teaspoon cracked black peppercorns
½ cup grated Parmesan cheese
2 tablespoons red wine vinegar

2 tablespoons fresh lime or lemon juice
3 dashes of Tabasco
1 dash of Worcestershire sauce
1 egg (optional)

---

2 medium heads romaine lettuce
1 cup seasoned croutons

1] Combine the anchovies, garlic, olive oil, and black pepper in a blender. Purée until smooth. Add the Parmesan cheese and then purée briefly to combine. Transfer to a small mixing bowl.

2] Add the red wine vinegar, lime juice, Tabasco, and Worcestershire. Whisk and set aside. The dressing may now be refrigerated up to 2 days.

3] If using the egg, just before serving bring a small saucepan of water to a boil. Take an egg from the refrigerator and cook for 1½ minutes. Remove with a slotted spoon and rinse with cold water to stop the cooking. Crack open the egg and spoon into salad dressing. Whisk vigorously to combine.

4] Wash the lettuce leaves and dry. Break into bite-size pieces and place in a large salad bowl. Pour in the salad dressing and toss, a bit at a time, being careful not to leave a pool of dressing on the bottom. (Leftover dressing may be saved.) Scatter in the croutons, toss again, and serve.

Salsas and Condiments

IF YOU HAVE EATEN ONLY BOTTLED OR PREPARED SALSAS (SAUCES) AT HOME YOU ARE IN FOR A TREAT. HOMEMADE SALSAS ARE EASY TO MAKE AND THEIR FLAVOR IS FANTASTIC. ALL IT TAKES ARE A FEW GOOD INGREDIENTS, A WELL-SHARPENED KNIFE, AND A BLENDER TO PREPARE SALSAS AS GOOD AS THOSE IN ANY RESTAURANT—OR BETTER. SINCE THERE IS LITTLE IF ANY COOKING TIME AND ALMOST NO FAT INVOLVED, THESE SIMPLE SAUCES RELY FOR THEIR FLAVOR ON FRESH INGREDIENTS, SO DON'T CUT CORNERS. YOU'LL BE JUSTLY REWARDED BY THESE RELIABLE SALSAS—THE HEART AND SOUL OF THE MEXICAN KITCHEN.

MEXICAN SALSAS ARE USED AS SEASONINGS AT THE TABLE, WHERE THEY ARE SPOONED ONTO SNACKS, STIRRED INTO SOUPS, AND SPRINKLED OVER POULTRY, MEAT, AND FISH. IT IS OFTEN THE SALSA THAT GIVES MEXICAN FOOD ITS CHARACTERISTIC HEAT, SINCE THAT IS WHERE THE CHILES INEVITABLY ARE FOUND.

THE TYPICAL MEXICAN TABLE IS SET WITH TWO OR THREE KINDS OF SALSA—A FRESH RED OR TOMATO-BASED SALSA, A GREEN ONE WHOSE MAIN INGREDIENT IS TOMATILLOS, AND A SMOKY BROWNISH ONE MADE WITH A COMBINATION OF DRIED CHILES AND OTHER ROASTED INGREDIENTS. SMALL BOWLS OF CHOPPED ONION, CILANTRO, AND LIME WEDGES ARE ALSO SET ON THE TABLE JUST IN CASE DINERS WISH TO ENHANCE FOODS THAT ARE ALREADY HIGHLY FLAVORED.

SALSA FRESCA

This fresh chopped tomato sauce, also known as *salsa mexicana* or *pico de gallo,* is the most popular salsa in and outside Mexico. It makes a wonderful condiment for tacos, nachos, quesadillas, fajitas, and chips as well as grilled chicken, fish, and beef.

Although it may seem like a lot of chopping, do not try to save time by using the food processor or blender. The texture is meant to be rustic and chunky, not too liquid. Fresh salsa does not keep well, no more than one day in the refrigerator. This is a good quantity for a large party—you may want to cut it in half for a smaller gathering.

✘ *Makes 4½ cups*

3 large ripe tomatoes, with skins and seeds
½ red onion, diced
1 or 2 serrano chiles, with seeds and veins, finely diced
½ cup chopped fresh cilantro leaves

2 tablespoons lime juice (about 1 lime)
¼ teaspoon salt
2 dashes of Tabasco, or more to taste

Remove the cores and finely chop the tomatoes. Place in a mixing bowl with the remaining ingredients and combine well. Taste and adjust with salt, Tabasco, and lime juice. Chill until serving time, or up to 24 hours.

COOKED TOMATILLO SALSA

This spicy green sauce, or *salsa verde,* combines well with cheese, chicken, and pork in dishes like chilaquiles, chiles rellenos, and enchiladas. Use as many or as few of the chiles as you like, and if you prefer a milder sauce, discard the seeds and veins, which is where the heat is stored. ✗ *Makes 1¾ cups*

1 pound (about 14 small) tomatillos, husks and stems removed
½ teaspoon salt
1 medium white onion, roughly chopped
2 garlic cloves, roughly chopped

2 to 5 serrano chiles, stemmed and roughly chopped with seeds and veins
½ cup cilantro leaves, unchopped
1 tablespoon vegetable oil
1 cup chicken broth

1] Wash the tomatillos and place in a medium saucepan with enough water to cover. Add ¼ teaspoon of the salt and bring to a boil. Cook at a low boil for 15 minutes to soften. With a slotted spoon, transfer tomatillos to a food processor fitted with a metal blade.

2] Add the onion, garlic, serrano chiles, and cilantro to the tomatillos and pulse until the mixture is a slightly chunky purée.

3] In a large skillet, heat the vegetable oil over medium-high heat. Cook the puréed tomatillo mixture, along with the remaining ¼ teaspoon salt, for about 5 minutes to thicken. Pour in the chicken broth. Bring to a boil, reduce to a simmer, and cook, uncovered, 20 minutes, or until thickened to taste. (Thin the sauce with additional chicken broth if it thickens too much.) Store in a sealed container in the refrigerator up to 4 days.

FRESH TOMATILLO SALSA

The acidic quality of tomatillos is underlined in this minimally cooked table sauce—the green equivalent of salsa fresca. Use it as a dip for chips and for topping tacos. It loses its flavor and consistency quickly, so reduce the quantity if you won't be needing much.

✖ *Makes 2¼ cups*

1 pound (about 14 small)
  tomatillos, husks removed
1 small garlic clove
¼ medium white onion, roughly
  chopped
2 serrano chiles, seeds and veins
  removed, roughly chopped

¼ cup water
½ teaspoon salt, or more to taste
½ cup chopped fresh cilantro
  leaves

1] Wash the husked tomatillos and remove the stems. Place in a medium saucepan with enough water to cover. Bring to a boil, reduce to a simmer, and cook, uncovered, 5 minutes.

2] In a food processor fitted with a metal blade, with the motor running, drop the garlic down the feed tube to mince. Turn the machine off. With a slotted spoon, transfer the tomatillos to the food processor bowl along with the onion, chiles, water, and salt. Process until smooth, but do not worry about a few stray chunks of onion or pepper. They add authenticity.

3] Pour into a bowl, stir in the cilantro, and chill until serving time. May be stored in the refrigerator 24 hours.

ROASTED TOMATO SALSA

This salsa has a compellingly complex flavor for such an easy sauce. I love it with grilled steak or chicken and it is heaven on a plate of Huevos Rancheros (page 58). ✖ *Makes 3 cups*

6 medium tomatoes (about 2 pounds)
3 garlic cloves, unpeeled
½ medium white onion, roughly chopped

1 jalapeño chile, seeds and veins removed, roughly chopped
1 tablespoon vegetable oil
1 teaspoon salt

1] Preheat the broiler. Line a baking sheet with aluminum foil.

2] Remove the cores with a paring knife and place the tomatoes on the baking sheet. Broil, close to heat source, turning occasionally until skin is well charred, about 15 minutes. Set aside to cool about 15 minutes.

3] Heat a small, dry skillet over high heat. Toast the garlic cloves until the skins are charred and the garlic softens, about 7 minutes. Let cool.

4] Place the chopped onion, jalapeño pepper, and peeled garlic in a blender or food processor fitted with the metal blade. Pulse until finely minced. Then, when the tomatoes are cool enough to handle, remove and discard the charred skins by hand, working over the foil-lined tray to catch the juices. Place the tomatoes in the blender or processor. Carefully lift the foil and pour the tomato juices into the blender also. Pulse until a coarse purée is formed.

5] Heat the vegetable oil in a 10-inch skillet over medium-high heat. Pour in the puréed sauce and salt. Cook at a lively simmer, stirring occasionally, 5 minutes. Sauce may be reserved in a covered container in the refrigerator up to 5 days.

VARIATIONS. For a dressier version, stir in fresh corn kernels or toasted pine nuts for a minute or two at the end.

TOMATO AND CHILE PASILLA SALSA

■

This smoky table sauce was inspired by that of La Cabanita, a restaurant in Glendale, California. It is a nice change from the typical red and green table salsas. *✘ Makes 2 cups*

2 dried pasilla chiles, wiped clean
  with a damp paper towel
2 garlic cloves, unpeeled
¼ large or 1 small white onion
3 large tomatoes, roasted
  (page 5)

½ teaspoon salt
1 tablespoon vegetable oil
2 tablespoons chopped fresh
  cilantro leaves

1] Heat a cast-iron skillet or comal over medium-high heat. Toast the chiles until crisp and brown all over. Toast the unpeeled garlic cloves and onion quarters until evenly charred.

2] Trim and discard the chile stems and peel the garlic and onion. Chop the onion and chiles into large pieces.

3] Place the roasted tomatoes (with skins), chiles (with seeds), garlic, onion, and salt in a blender or food processor with a metal blade. Purée until slightly chunky.

4] Heat the vegetable oil in a small saucepan over medium heat. Pour in the puréed sauce and cook for 5 minutes. Stir in cilantro and let cool to room temperature before serving.

CILANTRO SALSA

This thin green sauce, similar to an Italian pesto or Indian chutney, balances well with fiery foods. ✖ *Makes 1 cup*

1 cup fresh cilantro, stems
   trimmed
1 jalapeño chile, seeded
¼ cup olive oil

Juice of 2 limes
Salt and freshly ground pepper
   to taste

Roughly chop the cilantro and mince the jalapeño. Mix with the remaining ingredients in a small bowl and serve, or reserve in the refrigerator up to 4 hours.

CHILE DE ARBOL SALSA

If you like that sensation of "Oh, my mouth is on fire and I think I'm going to faint!" this is the salsa for you. Serve to a macho crowd with plenty of chips, cerveza, and tissues for teary eyes. It comes from Laura Vera of the *Los Angeles Times*. ✖ *Makes 1 cup*

1 teaspoon oil
8 chiles de arbol, stems removed
1½ large tomatoes, peeled and
   seeded

½ small onion, diced
1 garlic clove, peeled and crushed
¼ teaspoon salt

Heat the oil in a small skillet and sauté chiles over moderate heat about 2 minutes, being careful not to burn. Transfer to a blender along with the remaining ingredients. Purée until slightly chunky. May be stored in a sealed container in the refrigerator up to 5 days.

QUICK RANCHERO SALSA

—■—

Ranchero or ranch-style Mexican cooking has come to signal rustic Tex-Mex dishes like this chunky tomato sauce. Serve it with breakfast foods such as Mexican scrambled eggs or Huevos Rancheros (page 58) or in enchiladas and chilaquiles. ✗ *Makes 2 cups*

2 tablespoons safflower oil
1 medium white onion, diced
1 green bell pepper, cored and
  diced
1 (28 ounce) can Italian peeled
  tomatoes

2 garlic cloves, roughly chopped
2 serrano or jalapeño chiles, veins
  and seeds removed, roughly
  chopped

1] Heat the oil in a medium skillet over moderate heat. Cook the onion and pepper until soft, about 10 minutes.

2] Drain the tomatoes and then crush over the sink to squirt out seeds. Put in the blender along with garlic and chiles. Purée until slightly chunky.

3] Pour the tomato mixture into the pan with the onions and simmer, uncovered, for 10 minutes. Serve hot. Finished sauce may be kept in a sealed container in the refrigerator up to 7 days.

PICKLED RED ONIONS

This typical Yucatecan garnish for pork, chicken, and beef is easy to make and keeps up to two weeks in the refrigerator. ✘ *Makes 2 cups*

1 medium red onion (about 8 ounces), thinly sliced
4 garlic cloves, slivered
½ teaspoon black peppercorns
¼ teaspoon fennel seeds

1 teaspoon dried oregano
1 teaspoon coarse salt
¼ cup cider vinegar
1 cup water

1] Bring a small saucepan of water to a boil. Add the onion slices, cook 30 seconds, drain, and rinse with cold water. Separate into rings with your fingers. Place the onion in a noncorrosive bowl, glass jar, or plastic container with lid.

2] Combine the remaining ingredients in the same saucepan and bring to a boil. Immediately remove from the heat. Pour over the onion rings. Cover and set aside at room temperature 1 day. Move to the refrigerator, where onions will keep up to 2 weeks.

EGG AND BREAKFAST DISHES

MEXICAN BREAKFASTS ARE NOT FOR THE FAINT-HEARTED. THE MORNING MEAL MAY CONSIST OF FRUIT OR JUICE, EGGS, TORTILLAS OR BREAD, CHEESE, REFRIED BEANS, AND SOME SORT OF MEAT OR CHICKEN—ALL LIBERALLY SPIKED WITH HOT CHILES—AND THEN WASHED DOWN WITH THICK, RICH HOT CHOCOLATE (PAGE 110) OR *CAFÉ CON LECHE* (COFFEE WITH WARMED MILK). OF COURSE, EACH OF THESE DISHES IS SUITABLE FOR LUNCH OR SUPPER FOR THOSE WHO LIKE TO START THEIR DIGESTIVE TRACKS OFF A BIT MORE TENTATIVELY.

Chilaquiles with Chicken and Tomatillo Sauce

This stove-top casserole of chicken, tortilla chips, and tomatillo sauce makes a delightful lunch or brunch dish served with a salad of tropical fruits and cinnamon-scented coffee or a fruity sangria. To make it even easier, you can prepare the salsa and the chicken the day before.

Serves 4

2 chicken breast halves with ribs and skin, about 1 pound
1 (14.5) ounce can chicken broth
6 corn tortillas
6 tablespoons vegetable oil
1¾ cups Cooked Tomatillo Salsa (page 48)
½ cup chicken broth from poaching
½ cup crumbled añejo or feta cheese

1] Poach the chicken by placing in a saucepan with the chicken broth and enough water to cover. Bring to a boil, reduce to a simmer, and cook 20 minutes. Transfer the chicken breasts to a plate to cool and save the broth in the pot.

2] While the chicken is cooling, cut each tortilla into 8 wedges. Heat the vegetable oil in a 10-inch skillet over moderate to high heat and spread paper towels on the counters for draining. Fry the tortilla chips in batches, being careful not to crowd the pan, about 1 minute per side, or until golden and puffy but not browned. Drain fried tortillas on paper towels to absorb excess oil.

3] When the chicken is cool enough to handle, remove and discard the skin and bones. Roughly chop the meat or shred into bite-size pieces. You should have about 1 cup of chopped chicken.

4] Preheat the broiler.

5] Pour off the oil from the skillet that was used for frying tortillas. Combine the tomatillo sauce, ½ cup broth from the poaching liquid, the chicken, and fried tortillas. Cook at a low boil for 5 minutes, until the chips are slightly soggy but still whole.

6] Transfer to a 9-inch round pie plate, cake pan, or ovenproof casserole. Smooth the top and sprinkle with crumbled cheese. Place under the broiler until the cheese begins to melt, not brown, 1 to 2 minutes. Bring to the table bubbling hot.

HUEVOS RANCHEROS

As much as I love this classic sunny-side-up egg dish, it is not the sort of thing I recommend serving to a crowd—too much last-minute cooking. On the other hand, what better way to prove your devotion to a beloved friend or mate than over a life-affirming breakfast of huevos rancheros and freshly squeezed orange juice? Make the sauce a day ahead if you have difficulty following directions in the morning.
✖ *Serves 2*

Vegetable oil, for frying
4 corn tortillas
4 eggs
1¼ cups Roasted Tomato Salsa
(page 50), warmed

2 tablespoons crumbled añejo or
mild feta cheese
2 tablespoons chopped fresh
cilantro leaves, for garnish
Freshly ground pepper

1] Pour vegetable oil into a small skillet to a depth of ¼ inch. Heat the oil, then fry the tortillas until lightly golden and barely crisp, about 1 minute. Set aside to drain on paper towels.

2] Spoon 2 tablespoons of the vegetable oil from the tortilla pan into a large skillet (nonstick if you have one). Place over medium heat and fry the eggs sunny-side up, all at once, until the whites are just set.

3] To serve, arrange 2 tortillas on each plate so they overlap in the center. Top each tortilla with an egg. Spoon the warmed sauce over the egg whites and tortillas, leaving the yolks showing. Sprinkle crumbled cheese over all and garnish with cilantro. Sprinkle some black pepper over the yolks and serve pronto.

SCRAMBLED EGGS
MEXICANA

Foods cooked mexicana-style are flavored with tomatoes, onion, and chiles. In Mexico, where they don't skimp on breakfast, this picante egg dish may come with a side of refried beans and some slices of toasted French bread or the delicious hard crusty rolls called *bolillos.* ✀ *Serves 4*

8 eggs
Salt and 3 dashes of Tabasco
2 tablespoons unsalted butter
1 medium white onion, diced
3 plum tomatoes, seeded and
  roughly chopped

2 to 4 serrano or jalapeño chiles,
  with seeds and veins, roughly
  chopped

1] Beat the eggs with salt and Tabasco in a mixing bowl.

2] Melt the butter in a 10-inch skillet over moderate heat. Cook the onion, tomatoes, and chiles until the onion is soft, about 10 minutes.

3] Pour in the eggs and reduce the heat. Cook slowly, scrambling and combining with a wooden spoon or fork, until the eggs are just set. Serve immediately.

EGGS WITH
CHORIZO SAUSAGE

—————————■—————————

Chorizo sausages are always removed from their casings and crumbled for cooking. Serve this hearty brunch dish with a basket of warm tortillas, along with bowls of sour cream and Salsa Fresca (page 47) for seasoning at the table. ✖ *Serves 4*

16 corn tortillas
3 chorizo sausages
1 tablespoon vegetable oil
1 medium white onion, diced

8 eggs
Salt and freshly ground pepper
Cilantro sprigs, for garnish

1] Wrap the tortillas in foil and warm in a 350 F oven for 15 minutes.

2] Squeeze the sausages out of the casings into a medium skillet or cast-iron pan. Cook over medium-low heat, crumbling the meat with a wooden spoon, about 5 minutes.

3] Push the meat to the edges of the pan and pour the oil in the center. Cook the onion in the center for about 5 minutes to soften, and then stir together the sausage and onion and cook about 3 minutes longer.

4] Meanwhile, lightly beat the eggs with salt and pepper. Pour into the pan, reduce the heat to low, and scramble along with the meat and onions until the eggs are just done. The Mexican style is for soft-cooked eggs. Serve immediately with warmed tortillas and cilantro garnish.

POULTRY, MEAT, AND FISH

My goal in choosing this small sampling of entrées is to reflect Mexico's rich regional heritage, while offering dishes that do not demand a lot of time in the kitchen or many special ingredients. There are light, grilled pork and chicken dishes as well as a few achiote-tinged foods from the Yucatan, a traditional mole from Puebla, a pumpkin-seed sauce from Oaxaca, Gulf Coast fish stew, and a couple of simple preparations for skirt steak that may be the quickest beef dishes you will ever cook. All are easy to enjoy with some warm tortillas and cold beer.

POULTRY

YUCATECAN GRILLED CHICKEN

Mixed citrus juices and freshly ground spices impart a wonderfully strong, tropical flavor to grilled chicken in this favorite from chef-owners Mary Sue Milliken and Susan Feniger of the Border Grill in Santa Monica, California. For an authentic Yucatecan meal, serve with Watercress, Jicama, and Orange Salad (page 43) and refried black beans (page 89). ✖ *Serves 6*

6 chicken leg and thigh pieces

MARINADE
6 tablespoons annatto seeds
1 teaspoon black peppercorns
2 whole cloves
12 large garlic cloves, peeled
2 cups freshly squeezed orange juice

1 cup freshly squeezed lime juice
½ cup fresh oregano leaves
2 tablespoons salt
1 teaspoon ground cumin
¼ teaspoon ground cinnamon

1] Prepare the marinade by grinding the annatto seeds, black peppercorns, and cloves in a spice grinder or coffee mill. For the best results, work in small batches. Make sure to clean your utensils immediately when working with annatto, since it is a powerful dyeing agent.

2] Turn on the motor of a food processor fitted with a metal blade. Drop the garlic cloves down the feed tube and finely mince. Then add the orange juice, lime juice, oregano, salt, cumin, cinnamon, and ground spices. Process 2 minutes. (The marinade can also be chopped and combined by hand.)

3] Place the chicken in a large glass or ceramic bowl or pan, pour in the marinade, cover, and refrigerate 8 to 24 hours.

4] To grill, bring a charcoal grill to a high fire and then cool down slightly. If using a gas grill, preheat at medium. Grill the chicken, skin side down, until the skin is crisp, about 7 minutes. Turn over and sear the other side. Then move the chicken pieces away from direct heat for slower cooking. If you are cooking over gas, reduce the flame to low. Cover grill and cook 15 to 25 minutes, keeping a careful eye and turning occasionally to avoid scorching.

CHILES STUFFED WITH CHICKEN, RAISINS, AND NUTS

This fragrant stewed chicken dish comes from a little home-style restaurant called La Cabanita, in Glendale, California. Chef-owner Maria Jimenez suggests you serve it along with black beans, a green salad, and flan for a typical Mexico City–style dinner party. Look for firm unblemished chiles for roasting and holding the filling. The chicken stuffing may be made in advance. ✖ *Serves 6*

3 pounds chicken breasts, with
   skin and bone
5 large ripe tomatoes, cored and
   scored with an X on the bottom
2 tablespoons vegetable oil
½ large white onion, diced, about
   1 cup
2 garlic cloves, minced
2 teaspoons ground pepper, white
   or black
2 teaspoons dried thyme
2 teaspoons ground cumin

1½ teaspoons salt
¾ teaspoon ground cinnamon
½ cup sliced almonds
½ cup raisins
12 large firm poblano chiles

GARNISH
2 cups sour cream
2 tablespoons chopped fresh
   parsley
¼ cup sliced almonds, toasted
¼ cup raisins, toasted

1] Place the chicken breasts in a large saucepan with enough water to cover. Bring to a boil, reduce to a simmer, and skim off the foam that rises to the top. Cook, uncovered, 20 minutes. Lift out the chicken and set aside to cool.

2] Meanwhile, place the tomatoes in a pan of boiling water and cook for 40 seconds, just to loosen the skins. Rinse with cold water, peel, and halve the tomatoes. Squeeze out and discard the seeds. Dice the tomatoes.

3] When the chicken is cool enough to handle, remove and discard skin and bones. Chop the chicken meat into small pieces.

4] Heat the vegetable oil in a large dutch oven over medium heat. Cook the onion and garlic until soft, about 5 minutes, and then stir in the spices: pepper, thyme, cumin, salt, and cinnamon. Cook, stirring constantly, until their aromas are released, about 2 minutes. Add the diced tomatoes, chicken, almonds, and raisins. Bring to a boil and reduce to a simmer. Cook, uncovered, stirring frequently, 30 minutes. (Do not be concerned if the mixture looks dry at the beginning. As it cooks down, the tomato juices will be released, making it a rich, moist stew with just enough liquid.) The chicken stuffing may be made in advance and stored in the refrigerator up to 2 days, or frozen 2 months.

5] Roast the chiles; peel and remove the seeds, following the same method as for Chiles Rellenos (page 96). As with chiles rellenos, try to make just one slit for cleaning and stuffing the chiles, but don't give up if the chiles do get torn up a bit. The dish will still have a wonderful taste.

6] Preheat the oven to 350 F. Lightly coat a 9 × 12-inch roasting or lasagna pan with vegetable oil.

7] Spoon the chicken stuffing into the chiles until they are well-stuffed and arrange, with the slits to the side, in the coated pan. Cover tightly with aluminum foil. Bake 45 minutes.

8] Serve hot with a simple topping of sour cream. For a more elaborate presentation, while the chiles are baking, toast the almonds in a 350 F oven for 7 minutes and toast the raisins in a dry skillet over a medium-low flame about 4 minutes, shaking occasionally. Sprinkle over the sour cream, along with chopped parsley, and serve.

MOSTLY ROSIE'S MOLE

Moles represent the perfect blending of Indian and Spanish cultures. Though there are hundreds of variations, they all share a depth of flavor brought about by the lengthy cooking of a complex combination of ingredients that may include dried roasted chiles, tomatoes, garlic, vegetables, fruits, seeds, nuts, spices, herbs, and sometimes, *but not always,* chocolate. The resulting dish is like a stew in which the sauce is the main ingredient.

This particular mole borrows a little from here and a little from there and is close in concept to a traditional *mole poblano.* The main idea is from a woman named Rosie who used to clean my friend Julie's house, with embellishments and refinements via another friend, Marianne, whose Mexican neighbor shared with her what she called *mole legitimo poblano*—or the one true mole from Puebla.

In any case, this is a good recipe for a reddish-brown, sweet, smoky mole that won't disappoint. Don't let the length of the recipe throw you. It's an easy dish to prepare, and the leftovers are lovely.

✄ *Serves 8* ☞

6 pounds chicken parts, preferably
   breasts and whole legs
3 dried California chiles
3 dried pasilla chiles
2 dried ancho chiles
2 large tomatoes
1 medium white onion, unpeeled
   and halved
½ cup raw unsalted peanuts
½ cup raw sesame seeds
2 whole cloves
¼ teaspoon aniseeds
4 garlic cloves, unpeeled

6 tablespoons vegetable oil
3 (1-inch) slices French, Italian, or
   white bread
2 ripe bananas, peeled and cut on
   the diagonal into thick slices
1 cinnamon stick
1 (3.1 ounce) tablet Ibarra
   Mexican chocolate, roughly
   chopped
24 corn or flour tortillas or French
   bread
Salt and freshly ground pepper

1] Wash the chicken and place in your largest stockpot. Add water to cover. Bring to a boil, reduce to a simmer, and cook, uncovered, 45 minutes. Remove chicken and reserve on a platter. Strain the broth and set aside.

2] Wipe off all the dried chile peppers with damp paper towels to remove dust. Place a dry cast-iron skillet over medium-low heat and lightly toast the chiles, turning occasionally, until fragrant, about 5 minutes. (The red California chiles will blacken and the others will turn glossy and lose some of their wrinkles.) Working over the sink, pull off the stems, shake out the seeds, and discard both.

3] Place the chiles in a large bowl. Bring a kettle of water to a boil and pour enough water over the chiles to cover generously. Set aside to soak and soften for 20 minutes.

4] While the chiles are soaking, turn on the broiler. Line a baking tray with aluminum foil and place the tomatoes and onion halves on the tray. Broil until charred all over (see page 5 for roasting techniques). Remove and discard the tomato and onion skins.

5] Combine the softened chiles (discard the soaking water) and roasted tomatoes and onions in a blender or food processor fitted with a metal blade. Purée until a thick paste is formed. Transfer to a bowl and reserve.

6] In the same cast-iron skillet, toast the following ingredients and then transfer each to the bowl of the food processor or blender. (It is not necessary to wash out the processor bowl since all of the ingredients will be recombined eventually.) Over medium-low heat, toast the peanuts and then the sesame seeds until golden, about 3 minutes each. Then toast the cloves and aniseeds together for less than a minute. Turn the heat to high and roast the garlic in the pan until the skins are blackened. Peel the garlic by crushing with the flat of a heavy blade and add to the combination in the food processor.

7] Heat 3 tablespoons of the vegetable oil in the same skillet and fry the slices of bread until golden on both sides. Remove and pour in 1 more tablespoon of the oil. Fry the bananas until golden. Break the bread into chunks and transfer with the bananas to the food processor. Pour in 1 cup of the reserved chicken broth and process until a loose paste is formed. Pour in the puréed chiles and process several minutes until a smooth paste is formed. (If you prefer a smoother, more refined sauce, you can pass the paste through a strainer, although it is not necessary. I prefer mine with a rougher texture.)

8] Heat the remaining 2 tablespoons of oil in a large heavy dutch oven over moderate heat. Stir in the puréed chile mixture, 3 more cups of the chicken broth, and the cinnamon stick. Bring to a boil, reduce to a simmer, and stir in the broken chocolate until smooth. Simmer, uncovered, about 30 minutes to thicken the sauce. (If you are preparing the sauce in advance, it can now be stored in the freezer or refrigerator. You will also have about 2 quarts of leftover broth from the chicken to store for later use.)

9] Wrap the tortillas in foil, or slice the French bread and warm in a 350 F oven for 15 minutes.

10] To serve, remove and discard the chicken skin, if desired. Place the chicken in the pot with the sauce and simmer over low heat, stirring occasionally, an additional 10 minutes, just to heat through and blend the flavors. Taste and season the sauce with salt and pepper. To serve, ladle chicken pieces onto plates and cover with lots of sauce, Mexican-style. Serve with plenty of warm tortillas or toasted French bread for mopping up the sauce.

TURKEY FAJITAS

Texas-born fajitas have gained so much popularity in recent years they are now even available in Mexico—at resorts catering to American tourists. Here, then, is my contribution to fajita history: low-calorie, low-cholesterol turkey fajitas—a very easy weeknight meal. ✗ *Serves 4*

12 ounces uncooked turkey breast, cut into thin slices

MARINADE
⅔ cup olive oil
⅓ cup lime or lemon juice
2 tablespoons chopped fresh marjoram or oregano
1 large garlic clove, chopped
½ teaspoon salt
¼ teaspoon cracked pepper

8 flour tortillas
1 tablespoon olive oil, for frying
½ red onion, thinly sliced
½ red bell pepper, cored, seeded, and cut in julienne

1 green bell pepper, cored, seeded, and cut in julienne
1 jalapeño pepper, with seeds and veins, minced
½ medium zucchini, cut in julienne
½ yellow crookneck squash, cut in julienne
2 tablespoons chicken broth
Salt to taste
Juice of ½ lime
½ recipe Salsa Fresca (page 47), for garnish
1 ripe avocado, roughly chopped, or Guacamole (page 39), for garnish

1] Wash the turkey slices and cut into 1 × ¼-inch pieces. Whisk together the marinade ingredients in a bowl or shallow pan. Add the turkey pieces, toss to coat, and cover with plastic wrap. Refrigerate 2 to 3 hours.

2] Preheat the oven to 350 F for warming the tortillas. Wrap tortillas in aluminum foil and place in the oven just before cooking the fajita filling.

3] In a large skillet, heat 2 tablespoons of the turkey marinade over high heat for 1 minute. Lift the turkey out of the marinade and toss in the hot pan. Stir-fry until opaque, about 1 minute. Remove the skillet from the heat and, with a slotted spoon, transfer the turkey pieces to a platter; discard the liquid in the pan.

4] Return the pan to high heat and pour in the tablespoon of olive oil. Fry the red onion, bell peppers, and jalapeño pepper until onion is slightly soft, 2 minutes. Add the zucchini and crookneck squash and stir-fry an additional 2 minutes.

5] Return the turkey to the pan along with the chicken broth and continue cooking and stirring 1 minute longer. Taste for salt, sprinkle with lime juice, and transfer to a serving platter. Bring to the table with salsa fresca and avocado or guacamole for rolling in warm tortillas.

ARROZ CON POLLO

An easy one-dish meal, rice with chicken is a staple family meal in most Spanish-speaking countries. A simple salad of bright, tart greens such as watercress or arugula would be refreshing with such a substantial main course. ✖ *Serves 4*

3½ pounds chicken parts, cut into about 12 pieces
Salt and freshly ground pepper
Paprika
3 tablespoons olive oil
1 medium white onion, diced
4 garlic cloves, minced
1 red bell pepper, cored, seeded, and cut into ½-inch squares
½ teaspoon ground cumin
¼ teaspoon ground coriander

2 cups canned Italian peeled tomatoes, drained and roughly chopped
1 cup chicken broth
2 bay leaves
¼ teaspoon saffron threads
1 cup long-grain rice
½ cup whole pitted green Spanish olives, stuffed with pimientos
½ pound large shrimp, peeled and cleaned

1] Preheat the oven to 375 F.

2] Wash the chicken pieces and pat dry. Sprinkle all over with salt, pepper, and paprika.

3] Heat the olive oil in a large heavy dutch oven over medium-high heat. Fry the chicken until browned on all sides, about 3 minutes per side, and transfer to a platter.

4] Reduce the heat to low. Sauté the onion, garlic, and bell pepper about 2 minutes, stirring constantly. Then add the cumin and coriander and continue cooking until the onion is soft and slightly brown, about 4 minutes. Use a wooden spoon to loosen and stir the browned bits from the bottom of the pan.

5] Add the chopped tomatoes, chicken broth, bay leaves, and saffron. Bring to a boil. Then stir in the rice, olives, and shrimp. Reduce to a simmer and return the chicken to the pan. Cover and cook 45 minutes, or until the rice is cooked through. Remove from the oven and let sit, with the lid on, about 15 minutes before serving. Fluff with a fork and serve hot.

MEAT

CARNITAS

Carnitas, crisp-fried pork bits, are one of the best fillings for soft corn tacos. Garnish with small chunks of avocado, diced red onion, a few cilantro sprigs, and a squirt of lime. Delicious! ✕ *Serves 6*

3 pounds boneless pork leg, shoulder, or butt, trimmed of excess fat
Salt
1½ pounds lard
4 garlic cloves, peeled and crushed

¼ teaspoon black peppercorns
2 marjoram sprigs
1 teaspoon salt
1 cup water
24 corn tortillas
2 avocados, cut into chunks

1] Cut the pork into 1½-inch cubes and sprinkle liberally with salt.

2] Melt the lard in a large heavy dutch oven over medium-low heat until it reaches 200 F.

3] Add the pork, garlic, peppercorns, marjoram, and salt. Simmer, stirring frequently, about 15 minutes. Then pour in the water and continue cooking, at the lowest possible simmer, about 2 hours, uncovered. Stir every 20 minutes or so to avoid uneven cooking.

4] Test for doneness by removing a piece of meat and tasting it. The meat is done when it is moist and juicy and flakes easily with a fork. Then turn the heat up to medium-high and cook the meat in the bubbling fat until it turns golden, but not brown, 3 to 5 minutes longer. Stay nearby and stir frequently since a moment or two can make the difference between pork that is moist on the inside and crisp on the outside and pork that is just dried out. Immediately transfer pork cubes with a slotted spoon to paper towels to drain.

5] Wrap tortillas in foil and warm in a 350 F oven for 15 minutes.

6] When pork is cool enough to handle, chop into small dice. Serve with chopped avocado and tortillas. Or reserve meat in a covered container in the refrigerator up to 4 days. To reheat, sprinkle with a few tablespoons of chicken broth, cover, and bake at 350 F about 15 minutes.

Mexican Cooking for Beginners

PORK WITH BLACK BEANS

This homey winter stew from the Yucatan was shared by Jana Green of Los Angeles. Serve it with warm corn tortillas. ✖ *Serves 4*

1 pound dried black beans
½ large white onion, peeled and
  quartered
2½ pounds pork loin roast
2 epazote or oregano sprigs
1 tablespoon salt
16 corn tortillas

GARNISHES_____
2 cups chopped fresh cilantro
  leaves
1 medium onion, diced
6 radishes, trimmed and sliced
2 limes, cut into wedges
Roasted Tomato Salsa (page 50) or
  Salsa Fresca (page 47)

1] Place the beans in a colander, rinse with cold water, and remove any dirt or stones. Place in a large heavy dutch oven, along with the onion, and fill with water to about 3 inches above the beans. Bring to a boil, reduce to a simmer, and cook, covered, 1 hour.

2] Trim the pork of excess fat and cut into 1½-inch chunks. Add to the bean pot, along with epazote or oregano and salt. Cook over low heat, covered, 2 hours longer. Stir occasionally and add water if the meat and beans seem dry. When done, the meat should flake easily with a fork and the beans should all be soft.

3] Wrap tortillas in aluminum foil and warm in a 350 F oven. Ladle stew into bowls and serve with warm tortillas and garnishes for guests to add at the table.

Poc Chuc

Poc Chuc, a traditional dish of lime-marinated pork cooked on the grill, is a fine example of the Yucatecan style—simple, clean, and light. This version comes from the Merida Restaurant in Pasadena, California. The traditional accompaniments are black beans, roasted tomato onion salsa, and grilled or pickled red onions. All you need is cold beer for an easy summer barbecue. ✖ *Serves 6*

2 cups fresh lime juice
6 garlic cloves, minced
4 pounds boneless pork shoulder,
    trimmed of excess fat and thinly
    sliced across grain
1 tablespoon coarse salt
ROASTED TOMATO ONION SALSA
1 medium white onion
3 large tomatoes

1 serrano chile
¼ teaspoon salt

---

24 corn or flour tortillas
Pickled Red Onions (page 54), or
    2 large red onions
Juice of 1 lemon
1 cup cilantro leaves, for garnish

1] Whisk together the lime juice, garlic, and salt in a large glass or ceramic roasting pan. Add the pork slices, toss to coat evenly, and cover with plastic wrap. Set aside to marinate in the refrigerator at least 2 hours, or as long as 8.

2] To make the salsa, preheat the broiler and line a baking tray with aluminum foil. Broil the onion and tomatoes (in their skins), turning occasionally, until charred all over, about 20 minutes. Set aside to cool.

3] Roast the serrano chile by holding with tongs over a gas flame until charred all over. Transfer to a small plastic bag. Seal and let sweat 10 minutes. When cool enough to handle, rub off the blackened skin and roughly chop with seeds and veins.

4] Remove the charred tomato and onion skins. Cut the onion into quarters. Place the tomatoes, onion, chile, and salt in a blender. Purée until medium chunky. Salsa may be stored in the refrigerator up to 2 days. Serve at room temperature.

5] Preheat the grill or broiler. Cook pork slices over medium to hot flames until lightly browned, about 10 minutes per side. Wrap the tortillas in foil and place over a cool spot on the grill for 10 minutes, turning once.

6] If you are not using pickled onions, grill the red onions. Cut into quarters and pull apart the layers to form small wedges. Place on skewers, sprinkle with lemon juice, and place on the grill with the meat. Cook until the edges brown slightly, about 15 minutes.

7] Transfer the meat and onions to a platter and garnish with cilantro. Serve hot with the salsa and warm tortillas.

PORK PICADILLO

■

Picadillos, sweet-and-sour minced meat preparations, are commonly used to stuff chiles for chiles rellenos, but they also make excellent tacos with some salsa fresca, chopped avocado, and cilantro.
✄ *Serves 4*

1 tablespoon vegetable oil
1 small white onion, diced
1 garlic clove, minced
1 pound ground pork
6 fresh or canned plum tomatoes, peeled, seeded, and diced
1 tablespoon tomato paste

¼ cup raisins
2 tablespoons cider vinegar
½ teaspoon salt
¼ teaspoon pepper
¼ teaspoon ground cumin
¼ teaspoon ground cinnamon

1] Heat the oil in a large skillet over moderate heat. Sauté the onion and garlic until soft, about 5 minutes. Add the pork, breaking it up with a wooden spoon, and cook until evenly browned.

2] Stir in the remaining ingredients. Cook over medium-low heat, uncovered, until all the liquid is evaporated, about 30 minutes. Adjust seasonings and serve with warm tortillas for tacos, or reserve for use as a stuffing for Chiles Rellenos (page 96). Picadillo may be stored in the refrigerator up to 2 days, or frozen for a month.

COCHINITA PIBIL

In authentic pibil cooking from the Yucatan, small pigs (*cochinitas*) or chickens are first marinated in a combination of achiote, spices, and citrus juices or vinegar. Then the meat is wrapped in fragrant banana leaves and steamed at low temperatures in a carefully built pit called a *pibe,* which is lined with leaves. The resulting food is tender, flaky, somewhat tart, and always mysterious.

The recipe here, adapted from the Merida Restaurant in Pasadena, is somewhat simpler. It calls for oven baking and achiote paste, available at Latin American markets. If banana leaves are unavailable, substitute aluminum foil rubbed with butter on the side facing the meat.

✖ *Serves 6*

MARINADE

3 large garlic cloves, peeled

½ small white onion, roughly chopped

2 tablespoons achiote paste

Juice of 2 large limes

1¼ cups cider vinegar

½ tablespoon salt

4 pounds pork leg or butt, trimmed of excess fat and cut into 1½-inch cubes

4 large banana leaves

24 corn tortillas

1] Make the marinade in the bowl of a food processor fitted with the metal blade. With the motor running, drop the garlic cloves and onion down the feed tube. Turn the machine off and add the achiote paste, lime juice, cider vinegar, and salt. Process about a minute to combine well.

2] Place the cubed pork in a glass or ceramic roasting pan, pour on the marinade, and cover with plastic wrap. Let marinate, in the refrigerator, at least 2 hours, or as long as a day. Turn the meat occasionally and spoon the marinade over all.

3] Preheat the oven to 350 F.

4] Generously line a medium glass or ceramic roasting pan with banana leaves so the leaves hang over the sides. Spoon the pork on top and pour on the marinade. Fold the leaves over and place one on top to enclose the pork. Cover tightly with aluminum foil. Bake 3⅓ hours. (You may want to place a large baking sheet on the bottom of the oven to catch drippings.) Wrap the tortillas in foil and place in the oven for 15 minutes.

5] To serve, ladle the meat and sauce into bowls. Serve hot with Pickled Red Onions (page 54) or chopped white onion, black beans, and warm corn tortillas.

BEEF TINGA

Tinga is a sweet and spicy stew of shredded beef seasoned with chorizo sausage and chipotle chiles. Like a Mexican brisket, it is easy to make, improves with a few days in the refrigerator, and makes a splendid filling for sandwiches or tacos. ✖ *Serves 4*

1½ pounds beef chuck
1 teaspoon salt
½ teaspoon black peppercorns
2 bay leaves
3 tablespoons vegetable oil
½ pound chorizo pork sausage
1 medium white onion, chopped
2 garlic cloves, minced
1½ cups reserved beef broth

2 cups canned chopped tomatoes
3 canned chipotle chiles en adobo
   sauce, chopped
½ tablespoon dried oregano,
   crushed
Salt and freshly ground pepper
Sour cream, chopped avocado,
   and chopped white onion, for
   garnish

1] Cut the beef into large cubes and place in a medium saucepan with enough cold water to cover generously. Add the salt, peppercorns, and bay leaves. Bring to a boil, reduce to a simmer, and skim and discard the foam that rises to the top. Cook, partially covered, 1 hour, or until the meat is tender. Set aside to cool in the broth and then strain and reserve the liquid.

2] When the meat is cool enough to handle, thinly slice across the grain on a diagonal so the meat falls into shreds.

3] In a large dutch oven or heavy saucepan, heat 1 tablespoon of the oil over medium heat. Remove the chorizo from its casings by squeezing and place the meat in the hot pan. Fry, crumbling the meat with a wooden spoon, about 10 minutes. Then push the meat to the edges of the pan and pour an additional tablespoon of oil in the center. Add the onion and garlic and fry, stirring and mixing with the sausage meat, until the onion is soft, about 5 minutes. Add the shredded beef with the remaining tablespoon of oil and briskly fry until the meat is brown.

4] Then pour in 1½ cups of the reserved beef broth, tomatoes, chipotles, and crushed oregano and mix well. Season to taste with salt and pepper. Cook, uncovered, at a gentle simmer, until the flavors are blended and concentrated, 15 to 20 minutes. Serve hot with sour cream, avocado, and onions for garnishing at the table.

CARNE ASADA

Skirt steak, a well-marbled, inexpensive thin cut with exceptional flavor, is a staple of Mexican cooking. Use freshly purchased steak rather than frozen to make perfect carne asada, since frozen meat may give up too much moisture in the pan, causing it to steam rather than quickly fry. Carne asada is one of the quickest and most popular fillings for tacos, or you can serve it with the classical accompaniments for carne asada tampiquena—rajas con crema, pinto beans, and guacamole. ✂ *Serves 4*

1½ tablespoons lime juice	Salt and freshly ground pepper
1½ pounds skirt steak	Olive oil

1] Squeeze the lime juice over the steaks and sprinkle them with salt and pepper to taste.

2] Lightly coat a large cast-iron skillet with olive oil. Heat over high heat 2 to 3 minutes. Fry the steaks, being careful not to crowd the pan, about 1 minute per side. Serve steaks whole with the traditional accompaniments suggested above, or slice thinly across the grain for tacos.

SKIRT STEAK WITH
ONIONS AND PEPPERS

—————◼—————

The sweet flavor of browned onions are wonderful with rich, well-marbled skirt steak. This is a very fast weeknight meal, served with some guacamole and soft warm tortillas. ✖ *Serves 4*

1½ pounds skirt steak
Salt and freshly ground pepper
2 tablespoons vegetable oil
2 white onions, sliced

3 garlic cloves, thinly sliced
2 fire-roasted (canned) green
   peppers, thinly sliced
2 teaspoons fresh lime juice

1] Sprinkle the meat all over with salt and pepper. Heat a cast-iron pan over high heat. Pour in the oil and give it a moment or two to heat up. Cut the steaks to fit the pan and then fry just until seared on each side, about 1 minute per side. (The middle should remain red.) Set aside to drain in a colander set over a plate.

2] Reduce the heat slightly to medium-high and add the onions. Fry, stirring frequently, until onions turn brown and start caramelizing. Add the garlic and pepper strips and continue frying another 5 minutes. (It is okay in such a rustic dish to slightly brown the garlic and blacken the onion in spots.)

3] Meanwhile, transfer the meat to a cutting board and thinly slice across the grain. Toss the meat into the pan and cook 1 minute longer, just to heat through and combine the flavors. Sprinkle with lime juice and serve.

GRILLED LAMB ADOBADO

Lamb's full flavor makes it an excellent carrier for such an exuberant chile-spiked marinade. Serve with an arugula or watercress salad and boiled new potatoes crisped on the grill for an easy summer barbecue. For taco making, just cut the grilled meat into slivers. ✖ *Serves 4*

2 pounds butterflied leg of lamb

MARINADE_____

5 garlic cloves, peeled
½ white onion, peeled and cut into 3 pieces
3 canned chipotle chiles en adobo sauce, plus 2 teaspoons sauce from the can
Juice of 1 grapefruit
Juice of 2 oranges
2 tablespoons apple cider vinegar
½ teaspoon ground cumin

¼ teaspoon ground cinnamon
1 teaspoon salt
½ teaspoon cracked black pepper
2 tablespoons chopped fresh oregano

_____

Olive oil
Corn or flour tortillas or rolls
Orange slices, lime wedges, cilantro sprigs, and chopped white onion, for garnish

1] Trim the lamb of excess fat and sinew. Cut into ¼-inch slices across the grain.

2] Make the marinade in a food processor fitted with a metal blade. With the machine running, drop the garlic down the feed tube to mince. Then add the onion and chipotle chiles and process until fine. Add the remaining marinade ingredients and process about 3 minutes to blend fully.

3] Place the lamb slices in a shallow ceramic or glass baking dish. Pour on the marinade to cover the meat. Cover with plastic wrap and refrigerate at least 8 hours, or as long as a day and a half. Remove from the refrigerator 30 minutes before grilling.

4] Preheat the grill or broiler. Brush the grate with olive oil. In a 350 F oven, warm the tortillas or rolls.

5] Grill or broil the strips of meat 2½ minutes per side. Arrange on a platter decorated with orange slices and serve with warm rolls or tortillas and bowls of chopped onion, cilantro, and lime.

SHRIMP WITH TOASTED
GARLIC SAUCE

If every sauce were as easy as this one, known as *mojo a ajo* in Spanish, the world wouldn't need cookbook writers. Just be careful not to overcook the garlic; it should be just a bit past lightly golden. This is also a great quick sauce for sautéed or grilled fish fillets. ✕ *Serves 4*

24 jumbo shrimps, with shells on, washed and dried
Olive oil
Salt to taste
4 tablespoons unsalted butter

4 tablespoons olive oil
8 large garlic cloves, cut into chunks
1 tablespoon fresh lime juice
Cilantro sprigs, for garnish

1] Preheat the broiler.

2] Butterfly the shrimps, with the shells on, by slicing them open along the inside curve and then pressing to lie flat. Place on the broiler tray, shell side up. Brush the shells lightly with olive oil and sprinkle with salt. Broil 4 minutes.

3] Meanwhile, melt the butter with the oil in a small pan over low heat. Add the garlic and salt to taste and gently cook, swirling the pan occasionally, until the garlic turns golden, 6 or 7 minutes. Keep a careful eye on the garlic, as it can turn brown and bitter in a matter of seconds. Swirl in the lime juice and remove from heat.

4] Place the shrimp, split side up, on serving plates, spoon on warm garlic sauce, and garnish with a sprig or two of cilantro. Serve hot with warm tortillas or French bread.

RED SNAPPER
TIKIN-CHIC

Mexican food isn't all chile peppers and refried beans. The cooking from the Yucatan, in particular, can be as subtle as any other. This unusual treatment for whole red snapper, from the Presidente Hotel on the Mexican Caribbean island of Cozumel, brings out the delicate flavor of fresh fish superbly. Serve with plain white rice to soak up the delectable juices. *Serves 4*

2 (2-pound) whole red snappers, cleaned
Juice of 1 lemon
Salt and freshly ground pepper
2 garlic cloves, peeled
½ medium white onion, roughly chopped
2 large ripe tomatoes, cored and roughly chopped
Juice of 2 grapefruits

Juice of 2 oranges (about 3 cups citrus juice total)
1 tablespoon achiote paste
1 tablespoon salt
1 teaspoon white pepper
2 tablespoons dried oregano
4 bay leaves
Thinly sliced oranges and tomato wedges, for garnish

1] Preheat the oven to 350 F.

2] Rinse the fish in cold water. Lay on a platter and sprinkle both sides with the lemon juice, salt, and pepper. Let sit 10 minutes.

3] Meanwhile, in a food processor fitted with the metal blade and the machine running, drop the garlic cloves and onion chunks down the feed tube. Then remove the cover and add all the remaining ingredients except the bay leaves and garnishes. Process until well combined; small chunks are okay.

4] Place the fish in a ceramic or glass roasting pan. Pour on the citrus mixture along with bay leaves and cover tightly with aluminum foil. Bake 30 minutes.

5] To serve, carefully lift out the fish with spatulas and/or large serving spoons and place on a serving platter. Ladle on about ¼ cup of the pan juices. They will mingle with the fish's juices to create a sauce. Garnish with orange slices and tomato wedges around the outside edges and bring to the table.

RED SNAPPER VERACRUZANA

This red snapper recipe—with its rustic, chunky sauce from the fishing city of Veracruz—is probably Mexico's best-known fish dish. This version is a bit toned down for American tastes. If you want to pump up the heat, retain the jalapeño's seeds and veins, or better yet, substitute hotter serrano chiles. ✕ *Serves 4*

2 pounds Italian plum tomatoes, or 2 cups canned
2 tablespoons olive oil
1 medium white onion, sliced
2 large garlic cloves, roughly chopped
1 jalapeño pepper, seeds and veins removed, diced
½ cup sliced green Spanish olives

1 tablespoon capers
2 bay leaves
1 teaspoon dried oregano
½ teaspoon salt
¼ teaspoon sugar
Freshly ground pepper
4 (6-ounce) red snapper fillets
Juice of 1 lime

1] To peel fresh tomatoes, bring a medium saucepan of water to a boil. Remove the cores, cut an X in the bottom of each, and plunge the tomatoes into boiling water for 20 seconds. Rinse with cold water. Peel, cut in half horizontally, and squeeze out and discard the seeds. Roughly chop tomatoes. If using canned peeled tomatoes, just remove seeds and roughly chop.

2] Heat the olive oil in a large skillet over medium-low heat. Cook the onion, garlic, and jalapeño pepper until the onion is soft, about 7 minutes.

3] Add the tomatoes, olives, capers, bay leaves, oregano, salt, sugar, and black pepper. Bring to a boil and simmer, uncovered, 15 minutes.

4] Meanwhile, rinse the fish fillets under cold water. Sprinkle with fresh lime juice. Place in the skillet, spooning the sauce over the fish to cover. Cover and continue to simmer 7 minutes longer. Serve the fish hot, smothered with sauce.

GRILLED TUNA WITH
CILANTRO SALSA

Uncooked salsas are exceptionally easy to prepare for outdoor summer entertaining. All you do is mix up the salsa while the grill is heating, toss a salad or boil some potatoes, and the meal is ready.
✖ Serves 4

4 (6-ounce) tuna fillets
Olive oil, for brushing
Salt and freshly ground pepper
1 cup fresh cilantro, stems
  trimmed

½ cup roughly chopped watercress
6 tablespoons olive oil
1 tablespoon plus 1 teaspoon fresh
  lime juice
½ teaspoon salt

1] Preheat the grill or broiler and coat the grate with oil. Lightly brush the tuna with olive oil and sprinkle with salt and pepper.

2] Make the salsa by combining the cilantro, watercress, olive oil, lime juice, and salt in a food processor fitted with a metal blade. Pulse just until a purée is formed, being careful not to process too long. (The blender will not work well for this. However all of the ingredients can easily be chopped and combined by hand for a slightly chunkier sauce.)

3] Grill or broil the tuna about 3 minutes per side for medium-rare. Serve topped with cilantro sauce.

RICE, BEANS, AND TORTILLA DISHES

MEXICAN COOKS ARE GIFTED AT COAXING FULL FLAVORS OUT OF SUCH HUMBLE INGREDIENTS AS CORN, RICE, AND BEANS—THE MAINSTAYS OF THEIR DIET. ALTHOUGH THESE MAY BE FOODS THAT SPEAK OF POVERTY ELSEWHERE, IN MEXICO NO ONE WANTS TO GO WITHOUT HIS DAILY SERVINGS OF BEANS OR WARM FRESH TORTILLAS.

RICE, WHICH CAME TO MEXICO VIA SPAIN, IS TRADITIONALLY EATEN AS AN ACCOMPANIMENT TO FISH OR MEATS. WHEN IT IS ELEGANTLY MOLDED AND GARNISHED WITH VEGETABLES AND HERBS, IT MAY EVEN BE SERVED AS A FIRST COURSE, CALLED A *SOPA SECA*, OR DRY SOUP.

BEANS ARE EATEN THROUGHOUT THE DAY—EVEN AT BREAKFAST—AND ALTHOUGH THEY ARE SOMETIMES SERVED AS AN ACCOMPANIMENT TO MAIN-COURSE MEATS, THEY ALSO ARE LAYERED INTO SANDWICHES AND COMBINED WITH CORN MASA IN A NUMBER OF CORN TORTILLA DISHES SUCH AS TOSTADOS, NACHOS, AND ENFRIJOLADAS. BEANS, WRAPPED IN FLOUR TORTILLAS ALONG WITH OTHER FILLINGS, BECOME OUR NORTH-OF-THE-BORDER BURRITOS.

MEXICAN HOUSEWIVES KEEP A POT OF BOILED BEANS ON HAND TO BE REHEATED OR REFRIED AT A MOMENT'S NOTICE. PINK PINTO BEANS ARE POPULAR IN THE NORTH, BLACK BEANS IN CENTRAL AND SOUTHERN REGIONS SUCH AS OAXACA AND THE YUCATAN. IF YOU CAN'T TAKE THE TIME TO MAKE BEANS FROM SCRATCH, MEXICAN FOOD COMPANIES MAKE DECENT BEANS BOTH PLAIN AND REFRIED, WITH OR WITHOUT LARD.

MEXICAN RICE

———————— ■ ————————

This red rice is the standard accompaniment, along with beans, to many Mexican foods. The Mexican technique of first frying rice and then cooking it in a flavorful purée—in this case tomato—is an easy way to add flavor and texture to ordinary white rice. ✕ *Serves 4*

1 ripe medium tomato, cored and
   chopped
½ small onion, chopped
2 garlic cloves, peeled
2 tablespoons vegetable oil
1 cup long-grain white rice

½ teaspoon salt
¼ teaspoon ground cumin
⅛ teaspoon white pepper
Pinch of ground cinnamon
1½ cups chicken broth

1] Combine the tomato, onion, and garlic in a blender. Purée until smooth.

2] In a medium saucepan, with lid, heat the oil over medium-high heat. Add the rice and fry, stirring frequently, until opaque and golden.

3] Pour in the tomato purée, salt, cumin, white pepper, and cinnamon and continue cooking, stirring frequently, until most of the liquid is absorbed. Pour in the chicken broth. Bring to a boil, reduce to a simmer, and cover. Cook 25 minutes, or until the liquid is absorbed. Let sit with the cover on 10 minutes longer. Fluff and serve.

VARIATIONS. To serve as a traditional second course, or *sopa seca*, garnish with avocado slices and some chopped parsley or cilantro. Or, for a more substantial accompaniment, stir one (10-ounce) package of thawed frozen peas into the finished rice.

GREEN RICE

The wonderful herbal aroma and assertive flavor of green rice make it a good match for Yucatecan Grilled Chicken (page 63) or other strong, plain foods. ✖ *Serves 4*

1 fire-roasted (canned) Anaheim chile, chopped
1 cup roughly chopped fresh cilantro leaves
½ cup roughly chopped fresh parsley leaves
2 scallions, white and green parts, sliced

1 garlic clove, crushed and peeled
2 tablespoons vegetable oil
1 cup long-grain white rice
½ teaspoon ground cumin
¼ teaspoon ground coriander
2 cups chicken broth
½ teaspoon salt

1] Combine the Anaheim chile, cilantro, parsley, scallions, and garlic in a food processor fitted with the metal blade or blender. Purée.

2] In a medium saucepan, heat the oil over medium-high heat. Fry the rice until golden and opaque, stirring frequently, about 4 minutes. Add the puréed herbs, cumin, and coriander and reduce the heat to low. Cook, stirring frequently to avoid scorching, about 2 minutes.

3] Pour in the broth and salt and bring to a boil. Reduce to a simmer, cover, and cook 25 minutes. Turn off the heat and let sit, with the cover on, 10 minutes longer. Fluff with a fork and serve hot.

RICE PILAF
WITH SAFFRON
AND PINE NUTS

Saffron-scented rice adds a touch of Spanish elegance to fish and chicken entrées. Although it is quite expensive, do not use anything but real saffron in recipes calling for it. A small quantity goes a long way, and nothing else has the same distinctive aroma and flavor. ✗ *Serves 4*

2 tablespoons safflower oil
1 medium white onion, diced
1 small garlic clove, minced
1 cup long-grain white rice

⅛ teaspoon saffron threads
2 cups chicken broth
1 teaspoon salt
½ cup pine nuts

1] Heat the oil in a medium saucepan over moderate heat. Sauté the onion, garlic, and rice, stirring frequently to prevent scorching, until the onion is translucent and the rice is opaque and golden.

2] Stir the saffron into the chicken broth and pour into the pan along with the salt. Bring to a boil, reduce to a simmer, and cover. Cook 20 minutes.

3] Meanwhile, heat the oven to 325 F. Spread the pine nuts on a cookie sheet and bake, shaking the pan occasionally, until nuts are lightly browned, about 7 minutes.

4] When the rice is done, stir in the toasted pine nuts and put the cover back on. Let sit, off the heat but with the cover on, 10 minutes. Fluff and serve.

BEANS

BEANS IN THE POT

■

I avoided cooking beans for years until I learned that all that presoaking stuff was unnecessary—probably some kind of conspiracy by the home economists to get us to plan our meals in advance. Beans really need to be boiled only for a few hours, and then, without much intervention from the cook, they are ready to be eaten by themselves, over plain white rice, refried, or puréed for soup. The only trick to keep in mind is not to add the salt until the end of cooking time to keep the beans soft. ✖ *Makes 8 cups*

1 pound dried black or pinto beans
1 medium white onion, peeled
    and quartered
1 small head garlic

2 epazote or oregano sprigs
    (optional)
1 tablespoon salt, or more to taste

1] Clean the beans by placing in a colander and rinsing with cold water. Look over and pick out any stones or debris mixed in the beans.

2] Place the beans in a large heavy saucepan or dutch oven with the quartered onion. Slice off and discard the top and bottom of the garlic head, exposing the tips. Add to the bean pot. Pour in enough water to rise above the beans by 3 inches. Add the epazote or oregano sprigs, if desired.

3] Bring to a boil, reduce to a simmer, and cook, partially covered, 2 to 3 hours, or until the smallest bean is soft inside. Stir in the salt and cook an additional 10 minutes. Serve strained, or with as much broth as you like. Save leftover beans, in their broth, in a covered container in the refrigerator as long as 2 weeks.

REFRIED BEANS

This classic accompaniment can be made in advance and reheated as needed, along with a bit of chicken broth if necessary to thin it out. It also freezes well. ✖ *Serves 4 as an accompaniment*

2 tablespoons butter, lard, or
   vegetable oil
¾ cup diced white onion
3 cups unstrained boiled black or
   pinto beans, in their cooking
   liquid

Salt
½ cup crumbled añejo or feta
   cheese (optional)

1] Melt the butter or lard or heat the oil in a 10-inch skillet over moderate heat. Fry the onion until lightly browned, 5 to 7 minutes.

2] Add the beans and broth. Reduce the heat to low and cook, stirring frequently and crushing the beans with the back of a wooden spoon until a coarse paste is formed, about 15 minutes. Season to taste with salt and sprinkle with cheese, if desired. Serve hot.

HOMEMADE CORN TORTILLAS

——————————■——————————

Homemade tortillas are thicker and more cakey than the perfectly symmetrical ones available at the market. Though they are definitely not an everyday thing, they do add a wonderful personal touch to parties—especially if you are entertaining with a partner or have help in the kitchen. The best way to eat them is hot off the griddle, so be prepared for plenty of milling around in the kitchen. The earthy aroma of freshly toasted corn tortillas can be habit-forming. ✖ *Makes 8 (4-inch) tortillas*

1 cup Quaker Oats brand masa harina (page 11)

½ cup warm water

1] Preheat a heavy cast-iron skillet, griddle, or *comal* over high heat about 15 minutes.

2] Place masa harina in a mixing bowl. Add water and stir with a wooden spoon to combine. Then press together by hand to form a moist, smooth ball of dough. If dough does not hold together, sprinkle with additional water, a bit at a time. Or if dough is too sticky, sprinkle with masa. This should be an easy dough to handle.

3] Divide the dough into 8 equal pieces and roll each between moistened palms to form small balls. Set aside and cover with plastic wrap to prevent drying until skillet is ready.

4] When the skillet is ready, start pressing out the tortillas one at a time. Open the tortilla press and line the bottom with a heavy plastic sandwich bag. Flatten a dough ball slightly between your palms and place on top of the plastic in the center of the press. Cover with another plastic bag and press down the top of tortilla press. Press the handle firmly twice to flatten dough. Lift the cover and peel away the top plastic bag. Then, holding the corner of the remaining plastic bag, flip the tortilla, dough side down, onto the palm of your other hand. Peel off the remaining plastic bag and quickly slap the tortilla onto the hot griddle.

5] Cook about 20 seconds, until the edges begin to darken. Turn over with a spatula and cook the second side about 40 seconds longer, pressing with the spatula once or twice, until the tortilla begins to puff. Flip over and cook 10 seconds longer. Stack the finished tortillas on a cotton towel and wrap to keep warm. If not serving immediately, wrap well in aluminum foil and store in the refrigerator or freezer.

To reheat, wrap in foil and warm in a 350 F oven 15 minutes, as you would packaged tortillas.

TORTILLA CHIPS AND TOSTADA SHELLS

Packaged corn chips are a pale second to warm, homemade tortilla chips, or *totopos*. Along with table salsas and fresh tortillas, they are the measure of a really good Mexican restaurant. Homemade chips can be fried in advance and stored in a paper bag for a few hours. To reheat, just spread them out on a baking sheet in a 200 F oven for about 10 minutes.

Store-bought corn tortillas, regular size

Vegetable or corn oil
Salt for sprinkling (optional)

1] Tortillas fry better if they have dried out some first—old tortillas are perfect for frying. Let them sit, out of the package, on a counter for 30 minutes before frying.

2] Pour ½ inch of oil into an 8-inch skillet. Heat over moderate heat about 4 minutes. Line the counters with paper towels.

3] For chips, cut each tortilla into 6 wedges; leave tortillas whole for tostada shells. Test the oil by frying one chip. If bubbles form immediately and the tortilla puffs slightly and turns golden, not brown, the oil is ready. Adjust the heat accordingly. Fry the chips a handful at a time, being careful not to crowd the pan, about 45 seconds per side, turning with tongs. Transfer to paper towels to drain and sprinkle with salt, if desired. Follow the same procedure, keeping the tortillas whole, for tostadas.

CHICKEN ENCHILADAS
IN TOMATILLO SAUCE

Although enchilada literally means "dipped in chile sauce," the name has come to refer to a wide variety of corn masa dishes—all involving a corn tortilla rolled around a filling and topped or dipped in a sauce. This particular version is light and easy and makes a nice small supper. ✄ *Makes 12 enchiladas, serves 4 as an entrée*

2 pounds chicken breasts with skin
   and bone (about 2 whole
   breasts)
¼ cup diced white onion
¾ cup plain yogurt
Salt and freshly ground pepper
Vegetable oil

12 corn tortillas
Cooked Tomatillo Salsa
   (page 48)
½ cup sour cream
⅔ cup crumbled añejo or feta
   cheese
Cilantro sprigs, for garnish

1] Place chicken breasts in a large saucepan, cover with water, and bring to a boil. Reduce to a simmer and cook, uncovered, 20 minutes. Let cool in the broth.

2] When the chicken has cooled, remove and discard the skin and bones. Shred or finely chop the meat. Place the chicken in a medium saucepan with onion, yogurt, salt, and pepper. Cook over low heat, stirring frequently, until soft and moist, 5 to 10 minutes.

3] Soften the tortillas by quick-frying: In a small saucepan, pour oil to a depth of ¼ inch. Heat over medium-low. Quickly fry the tortillas, one at a time, about 10 seconds per side. Set aside to drain on paper towels and pat the tops to absorb as much oil as possible.

4] Assemble the enchiladas as follows: Place 2 heaping tablespoons of chicken filling in the center of each tortilla and roll to enclose. Transfer to serving plates, seam side down, 3 to a plate for dinner portions. Divide the salsa and ladle over the tortillas. Top each serving with a dollop of sour cream and sprinkle with añejo or feta cheese. Garnish with cilantro sprigs and serve.

VEGETABLES

THE MEXICAN KITCHEN DOES NOT HAVE A LARGE REPERTOIRE OF VEGETABLE SIDE DISHES. INSTEAD, VEGETABLES AND FRESH HERBS ARE LIBERALLY INCORPORATED INTO SUCH STEWS AS POZOLES AND MOLES, PURÉED INTO SOUPS, PICKLED INTO SNACK FOODS, AND CHOPPED TO MAKE SALSAS AND SMALL SALADS FOR GARNISHING TACOS AND OTHER ANTOJITOS. EXCEPT FOR CHILES RELLENOS, WHICH IS SUBSTANTIAL ENOUGH TO SERVE AS A MAIN COURSE, THE VEGETABLE RECIPES THAT FOLLOW ARE FOR SIDE DISHES. ALL ARE QUICK, EASY WAYS TO BRING AN AUTHENTIC MEXICAN FLAVOR TO YOUR TABLE.

RAJAS CON CREMA

These strips of hot chiles in a coating of cream are a traditional rich accompaniment to Carne Asada (page 76). They are also wonderful wrapped in warm corn tortillas or on top of the cornmeal cakes called *sopes.* They can be made in advance and reheated without any loss of quality. ✖ *Serves 4 to 6*

6 large, fresh poblano chiles
2 tablespoons olive oil
1 medium white onion, thinly
    sliced
2 large garlic cloves, slivered
½ teaspoon salt

½ cup heavy cream
½ teaspoon dried oregano
Juice of ½ lime
¼ cup crumbled añejo or feta
    cheese

1] Roast the chiles (as described on page 8) over a high gas flame or under an electric broiler until entirely blackened. Transfer to a plastic bag, seal with a knot, and let steam about 15 minutes. Working over the sink, rub off blackened skin and rinse lightly with cold water. Cut out and discard the cores, seeds, stems, and large veins. Slice lengthwise into ¼-inch strips.

2] Heat the olive oil in a medium skillet over moderate heat. Sauté the onion, garlic, and salt until the garlic is slightly golden, about 6 minutes. Add the roasted chile strips, reduce the heat to low, and cook, stirring occasionally, 2 minutes longer.

3] Pour in the cream and oregano. Turn the heat to medium and let the cream bubble until thick enough to thickly coat the vegetables. Remove from heat. Sprinkle with lime juice and cheese. Stir to soften the cheese and combine the flavors. Bring to the table hot.

CHILES RELLENOS

S tuffed chiles are a mainstay of the Mexican diet. These hearty poblanos stuffed with cheese are satisfying enough to serve as a light supper. The milder Anaheim or California chiles may be substituted, although they are not as tasty or as easy to stuff as the wider, thick-skinned poblanos. Never substitute canned chiles in a stuffed chile dish; their limp flesh will not hold up to stuffing and frying. ✖ *Serves 4*

SAUCE
2 cups Roasted Tomato Salsa
  (page 50)
½ cup chicken broth
¼ cup fresh corn kernels (optional)

4 large, fresh poblano chiles

½ pound Monterey Jack or white
  Cheddar cheese, at room
  temperature
3 eggs, separated
¼ teaspoon salt
¼ cup flour
Vegetable oil, for frying

1] Heat the sauce by combining the salsa with chicken broth and corn kernels, if desired, in a small saucepan. Cook at a simmer about 10 minutes and remove from heat.

2] Roast the chiles directly over a high gas flame until charred all over (see page 8). Be careful not to overcook, however, since you want the pulp to remain firm. If your heat source is electric, char the peppers under the broiler until evenly blackened.

3] Transfer to a plastic bag, seal, and let the peppers sweat 10 minutes. To peel, gently pull off the blackened skin by hand or by scraping with a small paring knife. Remove any stubborn spots by briefly holding under cold running water; be careful not to poke holes in the pepper and to leave the stems attached for stuffing.

4] To prepare for stuffing, cut one slit along the length of the pepper at a weak point in the flesh. At the very top, inside, under the stem, is the ball of seeds. Remove by cutting straight across at the base and then pulling it out with your fingers. The veins should remain intact. Just remove any stray seeds with your fingertips.

5] Cut the cheese into ⅛-inch-thick slices. Divide into 4 portions and stuff each chile with cheese. If the pepper doesn't quite enclose the cheese, you can seal it with a toothpick or two. The batter will also create a seal.

6] Just before frying, prepare the batter. Whisk the egg whites with an electric mixer or by hand until frothy, soft peaks form. Gently beat in the egg yolks, one at a time, with the salt, until just combined. Place the flour in a small bowl or plate.

7] Meanwhile, pour vegetable oil into a 10-inch skillet to a depth of ½ inch. Heat to 350 F. Line counters with paper towels for draining.

8] When the oil is hot enough for frying, coat the chiles, one at a time, as follows. (Do not do this step in advance as the batter is quite fragile.) First dip into flour and pat off excess. Then, holding with tongs, dip to completely cover with egg batter. Immediately transfer to the hot oil. Fry, 2 at a time, until golden brown all over, about 30 seconds per side. Transfer to paper towels to drain.

9] To serve, briefly rewarm the sauce and coat 4 serving plates with it. Top each with a stuffed chile and serve hot.

GRILLED CORN WITH CHILE AND LIME

███▪███

The primeval scent of charred corn hovers over the town squares, marketplaces, and street corners of Mexico, where vendors with portable grills sell this simple, satisfying food. Boiled corn pales by comparison. ✂ *Serves 4*

4 ears of corn, with silk and husks	3 tablespoons unsalted butter
¼ teaspoon chile powder, preferably New Mexican	1 lime, cut into wedges

1] Soak the unhusked corn in a large bowl or pot of cold water for 30 minutes. Meanwhile heat the grill.

2] Place the corn directly from the water onto the grill (do not wrap in foil) and cook, turning frequently until evenly charred, about 20 minutes. Remove from fire and, using a towel to protect your hands, fold back the husks and silk, leaving them attached at the stalk for easy handling. Return to the grill for 7 minutes, continuing to turn for even cooking.

3] Meanwhile, melt the butter with the chile powder. When the corn is done, transfer to a cutting board and chop into 2-inch lengths. Dip the corn in the melted butter mixture and serve with lime wedges for sprinkling.

SWEET CORN WITH CHILES AND CUMIN

━━━━━━━━━■━━━━━━━━━

Flecks of red and green peppers dress up fresh corn kernels in this easy side dish. ✖ *Serves 4*

4 ears of corn, husks and silk removed
1 medium Anaheim chile, seeds and veins removed
1 red bell pepper, cored and seeded

4 tablespoons unsalted butter
½ teaspoon salt
½ teaspoon ground cumin
Freshly ground pepper
Lime juice to taste

1] Remove the kernels of corn by holding the cobs, tapered end down, at a 45-degree angle to work counter. Using a sharp chef's knife or cleaver, run the blade from top to bottom along the rows to remove. Set aside.

2] Finely dice the Anaheim chile and red bell pepper.

3] Melt 3 tablespoons of the butter in a large skillet over moderate heat. Sauté the Anaheim chile and red pepper about 3 minutes. Add the corn kernels, salt, cumin, and a light sprinkling of black pepper. Cook, stirring frequently, 8 minutes longer. Stir in the remaining tablespoon of butter, squirt with lime, and serve hot.

Mexican Cooking for Beginners

DESSERTS

In the Mexican home, pastries and sweets are more often eaten with coffee between meals or as a snack in the late evening than immediately after the meal. Simple dishes such as flan and rice pudding suffice in most casual restaurants, while at the opposite end of the spectrum, dessert tables overflow with baroque Spanish-inspired creations in the more formal restaurants. The recipes included here are for the less fussy, familiar-tasting Mexican sweets: creamy puddings, cinnamon-scented brownies, tart lime and toasted coconut pie, and elegant mango ices. Each would bring a graceful close to any home-cooked meal.

MANGO ICES

These ices can be dressed up with mint sprigs, a simple sauce of puréed raspberries, or sugar cookies for a more elaborate dessert—though the full taste of mango is wonderful all by itself.

Mangoes are so popular and abundant in Mexico—one of the world's largest producers—that they are sold sliced and skewered, as street food. *Makes 1 pint, or 4 servings*

½ cup water
½ cup sugar
2 pounds mangoes (about 2 large)
Juice of 2 limes
Grated zest of 1 lime
1 tablespoon fresh lemon juice

1] Combine the water and sugar in a small saucepan and bring to a boil, stirring occasionally. When the sugar has dissolved and the liquid is clear, remove from heat.

2] Using a sharp paring knife or serrated blade, peel the mangoes. Then make several slashes lengthwise through the flesh, down to the pit. Run a knife along the pit to remove the flesh. Chop roughly.

3] Combine the chopped mango, lime juice, zest, and lemon juice in a food procesor fitted with the steel blade. Purée several minutes until smooth. Pour in the sugar syrup and briefly process to combine.

4] Pour the mixture into a bowl or plastic container and store, covered, in the refrigerator until well chilled, about 3 hours.

5] Pour into an ice cream maker and follow manufacturer's instructions for making sherbet. When finished churning, transfer to a plastic container and store in the freezer for a couple of hours for the flavors to ripen before serving. Homemade ices keep in the freezer up to 1 week.

FLAN

■

Flan, one of the all-time great comfort foods from Spain, is perfect for entertaining since it can be made well in advance. When working with caramel, it is important to work quickly since it hardens in a minute or two. ✘ *Serves 10*

CARAMEL	6 egg yolks
1½ cups sugar	1 cup sugar
½ cup water	1 quart half-and-half
	⅓ cup rum
4 whole eggs	1 teaspoon vanilla extract

1] Preheat the oven to 325 F. Have ready 10 (½ cup) ovenproof ramekins or one 9-inch round cake pan and 2 roasting pans.

2] To make the caramel: Combine the sugar and water in a light-colored skillet or saucepan over moderate heat. (The light color makes it easier to see the sugar change color.) Bring to a boil and cook until the sugar melts and the liquid starts browning, or caramelizing. Then reduce the heat to low and continue cooking 10 to 15 minutes, until the syrup is medium to deep brown, with the distinctive aroma of caramel. Do not stir the caramel as it is cooking or it will stick to the spoon. Instead swirl the pan occasionally and brush down the sides with a pastry brush dipped in cold water.

Since caramel sets quickly, immediately pour the hot liquid into the ramekins or cake pan and swirl to coat the bottoms and sides. Set ramekins inside 2 roasting pans (or cake pan in one) and make the custard.

3] In a large mixing bowl, gently whisk together the eggs, egg yolks, sugar, half-and-half, rum, and vanilla. Using a ladle, pour the custard into caramel-coated molds.

4] Bring a large kettle of water to a boil. Place the roasting pans with custard cups on a surface close to the oven, since they will soon be very heavy. Pour the boiling water into the pans so the water rises halfway up the sides of the ramekins. (This is called making a water bath, or *bain marie*. It ensures even cooking and prevents the bottom and sides from browning.)

5] Bake, uncovered, 1 hour to 1 hour 15 minutes. To test for doneness, dip a paring knife into the center of a flan. (If you are baking on 2 racks, it is best to test one from each pan since temperatures and cooking times will vary.) If the tip comes out clean, without particles sticking to it, it is done. Remove from oven and, using pot holders, transfer the cups to counters to cool to room temperature. Cover with plastic wrap touching the tops and chill until serving time. Flan keeps in the refrigerator up to 5 days.

6] To serve, run a paring knife between the custard and the mold. Invert onto dessert plates, shake to loosen, and scrape out and spoon extra caramel sauce over the top. If the custard sticks, plunge the bottoms into a bowl of hot water and then invert. (If you have trouble cleaning caramel-encrusted custard cups, place in the sink and pour boiling water over all. Let sit until the water cools. It will dissolve the caramel.)

VARIATION. For coconut flan, lightly toast 1 cup grated, unsweetened coconut in a dry skillet. Stir into custard mixture along with the rum and vanilla.

MEXICAN RICE PUDDING

There are two things you can count on when dining out in Mexico City—flan and rice pudding on the menu for dessert. Mexican rice pudding is creamier and more liquid than our hard-baked version. It can be served hot or cold and can also be reheated, over gentle heat with a little bit of milk, for a wonderfully decadent breakfast porridge. ✗ *Serves 8*

6 cups water
¾ cup long-grain rice
1½ teaspoons salt
1 quart milk, whole or low-fat
¾ cup sugar
1 cinnamon stick
1 (2 x 1 inch) piece orange zest

4 egg yolks
¼ cup cold milk
½ cup raisins
1 tablespoon sugar with
    ½ teaspoon ground cinnamon,
    for sprinkling.

1] Bring the water to a boil in a medium saucepan. Add rice and 1 teaspoon of the salt. Cover, reduce to a simmer, and cook 15 minutes. Drain in a colander.

2] In a large heavy saucepan, bring the milk nearly to a boil. (When small bubbles form along the edges of the pan, the milk is scalded—or nearly to a boil.) Stir in the sugar, rice, cinnamon stick, orange zest, and the remaining ½ teaspoon salt. Bring to a boil and reduce to a simmer. Cook, uncovered, stirring occasionally, until thickened, 20 to 25 minutes. Remove from heat. Remove and discard the cinnamon stick and orange zest.

3] Whisk together the egg yolks and cold milk. Scoop about ¼ cup of the hot rice mixture into the yolks and whisk again. Then slowly pour the egg mixture into the pan with the rice. Stir in the raisins. Cook over very low heat, stirring frequently with a wooden spoon, 5 minutes longer. Remove from heat. Mexican rice pudding may be served hot, at room temperature, or chilled. It keeps, in the refrigerator, up to 4 days. Sprinkle with cinnamon sugar before serving.

PECAN BROWNIES

On the theory that one can never have too many brownie recipes, and since chocolate and pecans do come from Mexico, I have taken the liberty of including this moist, not-too-sweet brownie recipe here. It is seasoned with cinnamon—a common flavoring for chocolate in Mexico. ✖ *Makes 26 to 30 small brownies*

1½ cups pecan halves
4 ounces unsweetened chocolate
16 tablespoons (2 sticks) unsalted
    butter
4 large eggs
1 cup sugar
¾ cup packed brown sugar
1 teaspoon vanilla extract

¾ cup all-purpose flour
½ teaspoon ground cinnamon
¼ teaspoon salt
1 tablespoon ground cinnamon
    mixed with 2 tablespoons
    confectioners' sugar, for dusting
    (optional)

1] Preheat the oven to 350 F. Butter and flour a 9-inch square baking pan.

2] Toast the nuts by placing on a baking tray. Bake, shaking the pan occasionally, about 7 minutes. Set aside to cool.

3] Roughly chop the chocolate for quicker melting. Combine the butter and chocolate in the top of a double boiler or in a bowl placed over simmering water. Melt over low heat, stirring occasionally. Set aside.

4] In a large mixing bowl, beat together the eggs and sugars until smooth. Stir in the vanilla. Pour in the melted chocolate and butter. Mix until combined.

5] In a small bowl, mix together the flour, cinnamon, and salt with a fork. Add to the chocolate mixture and mix gently just until the flour disappears.

6] Chop the nuts into large chunks and stir into the batter. Pour into the baking pan. Bake 30 to 35 minutes, until a toothpick inserted in the center comes out clean. Set aside to cool in the pan, on a rack, for 30 minutes. Run a knife along the edges to loosen and remove from pan. Place the cinnamon and confectioners' sugar mixture into a small strainer and shake over the top to decorate, if desired. Cut into small squares.

ELENA'S CHURROS

Churros, deep-fried dough sticks dipped in sugar and cinnamon, are the Mexican equivalent of doughnuts. This recipe, adapted from the 1944 book *Elena's Famous Mexican and Spanish Recipes,* results in pastries that are much smaller and lighter than those sold by street vendors. Serve churros while they are still hot and I assure you these sweet little treats will not last the hour. ✖ *Makes 12 churros*

1 cup all-purpose flour
1 cup water
1 teaspoon salt
2 quarts vegetable oil

1 slice bread
½ lemon
¼ cup confectioners' sugar
¼ cup ground cinnamon

1] Sift the flour 3 times and place in a mixing bowl.

2] Bring the water with salt to a boil. Immediately pour into the flour and beat with an electric mixer at high speed until light and fluffy, about 5 minutes.

3] Meanwhile, in a 4-quart pot, heat the oil over high heat, along with the bread and lemon, until the bread turns nearly black. Remove the bread and lemon and reduce the heat slightly to medium-high. Line the counters with paper towels.

4] Transfer the warm, sticky batter into a pastry bag with a large serrated tip. Squeeze the batter, using a paring knife to trim, in 3-inch lengths into the hot oil. Fry, turning occasionally, until deep golden brown, about 4 minutes. Transfer with a slotted spoon to paper towels to drain.

5] Combine the sugar and cinnamon in a small brown paper bag. While the churros are still warm, transfer to the bag, seal the top, and shake to coat. Churros are best eaten within the hour.

BEVERAGES

MEXICAN COOKS BRING THE SAME LOVE FOR VIBRANT COLORS AND FLAVORS TO THEIR DRINKS AS THEY DO TO THE REST OF THE MEAL. THESE BEVERAGES CAN ALL BE MADE IN A SNAP AND ARE A VAST IMPROVEMENT OVER SOFT DRINKS OR PACKAGED FRUIT JUICES. ON THE OTHER HAND, SERVING COLD BEER WITH LIME WEDGES IS PRETTY EASY ALSO.

Limeade

The few minutes it takes to dissolve the sugar by boiling makes the difference between a so-so limeade and a transcendent one. Perfect for summer entertaining, limeade mixes well with most Mexican flavors. You can also use this method for making wonderful homemade lemonade. *Makes 1½ quarts*

¾ cup sugar
7½ cups water
¾ cup lime juice (juice of about 10 limes)
1 lime, washed and sliced

1] Make a syrup by combining the sugar with ¾ cup of the water in a small heavy saucepan. Cook at a low boil, stirring occasionally, until the sugar dissolves and the liquid is clear, about 3 minutes.

2] Pour into a pitcher and combine with the lime juice and 6¾ cups of water. Stir well, garnish with lime slices, and chill. Serve over ice cubes.

Fruit Milk Shake

Mexican juice bars are a tempting sight, with their brilliantly colored tropical fruits in the window and blenders lined up on the counter ready to perform their magic. In addition to a wide variety of fruit juices mixed with water or milk, juice bars usually sell foods that can be eaten on the run—tacos, tortas, and empanadas. This milk shake, known as a *liquado,* makes a healthful midafternoon snack. *Serves 1*

¾ cup washed, peeled fruit, such as mangoes, bananas, strawberries, pineapple, peaches
1 cup milk
½ tablespoon or more sugar

1] Clean the fruit, removing any skin, stems, or tough fibers. Chop into chunks, reserving any juice.

2] Place fruit with juices in a blender and purée until smooth. Pour in the milk and sugar and liquefy at high speed until smooth and frothy, about 30 seconds. Taste and adjust with sugar as necessary. Serve in a tall glass with ice cubes.

MEXICAN HOT CHOCOLATE

Hot chocolate, considered a sacred drink by the Aztecs, was brought back to Europe by Cortez in the sixteenth century, where it quickly became a favorite of the upper classes. Mexican chocolate, pre-sweetened and flavored with cinnamon and ground almonds, makes an especially luxurious beverage. ✗ *Serves 2*

1 (3.1-ounce) tablet Ibarra chocolate	2 cups milk

Chop the chocolate roughly and place in a small saucepan with the milk. Bring barely to a boil, stirring now and then to dissolve the chocolate. When bubbles appear on the surface, pour into a blender and whir at high speed until frothy, about 40 seconds. (Chocolate can also be beaten by hand with a whisk or the wooden *molinillo*, made for that purpose and sold at ethnic markets.) Serve in large mugs or glasses.

DOUG'S MARGARITAS

This elegantly spare margarita recipe, from Doug Bergstresser, remains faithful to the original, as conceived by Mexican hotelier and restaurateur Danny Herrera in the late 1940s. According to legend, he named it for an American actress named Marjorie, who was visiting his hotel. It seems she had a terrible thirst and was allergic to straight tequila. This is what he came up with. ✗ *Serves 2*

Ice cubes	2 limes
5 parts white tequila	Coarse or kosher salt
2 parts Triple Sec or Cointreau	

1] In a martini shaker or similar tumbler, combine ice cubes, tequila, Triple Sec, and juice of 2 limes. Reserve the squeezed lime halves. Vigorously shake until the mixture is ice cold and frothy.

2] Prepare the glasses by rubbing the rims with the lime halves to moisten. Place the salt in a saucer and dip the rims to coat. Place fresh ice cubes in glasses and pour in the shaken margaritas.

BOOKS ON MEXICAN CUISINE AND CULTURE

Bayless, Rick, with Deann Groen Bayless. *Authentic Mexican: Regional Cooking from the Heart of Mexico.* William Morrow, New York, 1986.

My favorite Mexican cookbook—for its clear design and organization, accessible home-style recipes, explanation of regional differences, abundant recipe variations, and all-around friendly style. To my mind, chef Rick Bayless and his wife, Deann, owners of Chicago's Frontera Grill, have done the best job yet of demystifying Mexican cooking for an American audience.

Cadwallader, Sharon. *Savoring Mexico.* Chronicle Books, San Francisco, 1980.

Cadwallader, a West Coast food writer with a taste for Mexico, took a long car trip through the country that resulted in this succinct travelogue with recipes. If you like practical, authentic recipes interspersed with descriptions of archaeological sights, cafés, and border crossings, this is the book for you.

Kennedy, Diana. *The Cuisines of Mexico.* Harper & Row, New York, 1972.

————. *The Art of Mexican Cooking: Traditional Mexican Cooking for Aficionados.* Bantam, New York, 1989.

————. *Mexican Regional Cooking* (revised edition). HarperPerennial, New York, 1990.

————. *The Tortilla Book* (revised edition). HarperPerennial, New York, 1991.

Englishwoman Diana Kennedy, who has been living in Mexico since the early 1970s, takes her job seriously as the doyenne of Mexican cooking. She is, after all, the expert the other experts turn to. Her densely packed books explore and explain every nuance of the true Mexican kitchen in patient detail. Though the recipes are a bit too authentic for my tastes (where do you shop for a cow's udder?), and the layout of the first book is too confusing, one never doubts for a minute that the author is writing from intimate experience and a deep well of passion.

Palazuelos, Susanna. *Mexico: The Beautiful Cookbook.* Collins Publishers, San Francisco, 1991.

This big, beautiful coffee-table book is also surprisingly useful. An informative text describes each region and its specialties, while the well-tested recipes run the gamut from rustic bean and tortilla casseroles to elegant Mexico City dishes such as *huitlacoche* (corn fungus) crepes. Gorgeous color photography captures the heart and soul, as well as the foods, of Mexico.

Quintana, Patricia. *The Taste of Mexico.* Stewart, Tabori & Chang, New York, 1986.

Cooking teacher and restaurant consultant Quintana takes the reader through her Mexico—the Mexico of elegant hotels, spas, and restaurants. Though the recipes are sophisticated enough to stand beside any upscale European cook's collection, this big, colorful coffee-table book feels much too formal to ever make the trip into the messy home kitchen.

INDEX